MW01272893

Learn 2 Invest Kid

The first book you should read
if you want to invest in blue
chip dividend paying stocks.
This is not taught in schools.

by
**Pavi Toor,
Jaiden Toor**
and
Pravin Toor

 FriesenPress

One Printers Way
Altona, MB R0G 0B0
Canada

www.friesenpress.com

ISBN
978-1-03-919791-6 (Hardcover)
978-1-03-919790-9 (Paperback)
978-1-03-919792-3 (eBook)

1. YOUNG ADULT NONFICTION, PERSONAL FINANCE

Distributed to the trade by The Ingram Book Company

Thank you Jasmine!

-Jaiden and Pravin Toor

Table of Contents

INTRODUCTION:
Young Guns Weightlifting and Boxing Club

"The people who succeed are irrationally
passionate about something."

— Naval

I was in another middle school gym, watching my son's basketball team lose again. It wasn't too bad; we only lost by thirty points this time. The students and parents were all used to this by now.

Over the years, I have noticed some basketball teams becoming physically stronger, especially in schools that have football programs. Many football players play basketball in the offseason. They aren't afraid of contact, and they lift weights to build strength. These kids play basketball on another level, like playing video games with a cheat code. They are faster, stronger, and score almost every time they shoot the ball. Our kids, trying to defend, just topple over like construction pylons.

Weightlifting did wonders for my athletic performance when I was a teenager. I initially started lifting weights to improve my slap shot in hockey. I also played basketball in high school, and lifting weights helped me with rebounding, especially when it got physical under the boards. Overall, I became stronger, faster, and more confident. Eventually, I stopped playing school sports and focused on weightlifting. Now, I thought it might be the right time to get my son to pump some iron.

I looked around and couldn't find any weightlifting programs for teenagers. Hiring a personal trainer seemed to be the only option available, but it was expensive. Private gyms are often too intimidating for young people. Most teenagers don't like to walk into a huge commercial gym where everyone is staring at them. This is a problem for many adults too.

We decided to strike out on our own and reserve gym space at a local recreation centre. We hired a personal trainer and encouraged kids from my son's basketball team to take part. It was free for the youth as we didn't want cost to be a barrier for the kids. They just had to show up. We started the program Young Guns in September 2019, a few months before the start of basketball season. We even got a university student to design our logo, just like Nike did! I'll talk more about this later.

Figure 1 - Our logo was designed by a local university student. That's all we could afford.

Young Guns Weightlifting and Boxing Club (Young Guns) is a free, coed fitness program for youth. Why is it called Young

Guns? People in the community liked the name when I initially proposed it, and it stuck. I did have to explain to a few people that the 1980s outlaw cowboy movie was not our inspiration for the club's name—the one where Emilio Estevez played Billy the Kid. One definition found online states that "young guns" is a term used to describe young people who have lots of energy, talent, and are expected to be successful. This definition was good enough for us.

Many communities struggle to get youth active, despite the many physical and mental health benefits of exercise. It also keeps kids out of trouble. After doing some research, we realized that some of the greatest limitations that youth face—when it comes to weightlifting—had to do with safety, inexperience, and a lack of financial resources. We created the club to provide free weightlifting training so that kids could learn how to lift weights safely and get results.

When it comes to weightlifting, youth should work with a certified trainer, or they could get hurt. There is a high risk of injury if proper instruction is not provided. Unfortunately, most kids who start lifting weights suffer from injuries because they don't know how to perform lifts with proper form. Every time I walk into a gym, I just cringe at seeing more than half the people there lifting incorrectly. Once someone gets injured, they usually quit. It can take many months to learn proper technique for compound exercises, such as bench press, squats, and deadlifts. Many beginners are not sure which exercises to start with.

We also discovered working out with a group is more motivating than lifting weights alone. We reserve an entire gym so that youth, particularly girls, can feel safe and not have to wait around for equipment while doing their circuit training. Have you tried bench-pressing or squatting during peak times at a regular gym? There is always a lineup. It could take up to an hour for the bench press to become available during peak times.

Most of our youth athletes compete at the provincial and national level in sports such as wrestling, basketball, football, soccer, boxing, and even hockey. These kids knew what it would take to get to the next level, but couldn't afford personal trainers, which is where our program came in. For example, hockey players require leg strength and power for agility and stability on the ice. Sidney Crosby—who became the youngest captain of a National Hockey League team and led the Pittsburgh Penguins to three Stanley Cup championships, as well as won two Olympic gold medals—relies on compound exercises, such as barbell squats alternated with barbell deadlifts, walking lunges, and plyometric box jumps, to build maximum strength. It's no surprise that Sidney's legs are like tree trunks and all muscle, contributing to his power and speed. We incorporate these same exercises in our program for our youth.

Young Guns trains four times a week and has certified trainers who coach up to twelve youths per session. We teach the basics of weightlifting and boxing. Young Guns fundraises through club merchandise sales to offset gym and trainer costs. We have sold over eighteen thousand dollars' worth of club merchandise since starting the club.

Figure 2 - Back in December 2019, we sold this package for $125 to raise money for our club. We raised $5,000 by the end of the month.

Figure 3 – Club members sold Young Guns T-shirts in November 2020. Since it was during the early days of COVID, there was no contact with customers. We received orders through our Instagram page and delivered them to the customers' homes.

We even sold high-protein donuts. They were made at a local bakery. Each donut had about five grams of whey and casein protein, which is almost as much protein as in an egg.

Figure 4 – These protein doughnuts were made at a local bakery. Because of COVID, we could not sell directly to the public. As a workaround, we took orders on our Instagram page, and customers paid us by e-transfer, picking the doughnuts up from the bakery. Those doughnuts got popular in the community.

ONE
Nonprofit or
Social Enterprise?

Nonprofits rely on fundraising activities, such as door-to-door sales and large formal galas, to fund operations. Meeting potential donors face to face is essential. Thanks to COVID-19 restrictions, typical fundraising activities were not allowed. We had to adjust our fundraising activities to the "new normal." Wearing masks and gloves, we packed our club T-shirts, then delivered them to customers. Orders for our protein doughnuts were received through the Young Guns Instagram page. Customers picked them up directly at the local bakery on Fridays and then e-transferred us the cash.

To make matters worse, many larger nonprofits, small businesses, and corporations also stopped making donations and approving grants because nobody knew how long the pandemic and the restrictions would last.

Royal Bank of Canada (RBC), our bank, is Canada's largest bank. In 2019, before the pandemic hit, RBC reported a record annual profit of $12.9 billion, which is $35 million per day. Even they stopped providing grants to organizations like ours during the pandemic. Just think about that for a minute.

Established nonprofits typically receive funding, while the new ones must fend for themselves. To qualify for most grants, you need to have several years of your organization's financial records and annual meeting minutes. It's easy to start a nonprofit, but getting funding is a whole different matter.

As of mid-2021, we had close to $8,500 in our bank account, thanks to merchandise and protein donuts sales. Our goal was to make enough investment income to fund our monthly club costs. We knew this wouldn't happen overnight, but we needed to take the first step. Leaving the money in a savings account in the bank was out of the question. The interest the banks paid was less than 1 percent, and the inflation rate was in the double digits. Everything was starting to get expensive, especially groceries and building materials (was everyone doing home renovations all at once?). We didn't need the money for at least a year. It was time to take a calculated risk and invest the money we had saved. If we didn't do anything, the club would have to close by the end of the year. Either we would end up making money or we would learn some valuable lessons.

Do you know the story of FedEx? In 1974, Fred Smith, the founder of FedEx, saved his company from bankruptcy by going to Las Vegas and gambling the company's last $5,000 on blackjack. He won $27,000, which was enough to keep FedEx going for another week. Smith then raised $11 million and kept the business going. Two years later, FedEx made its first profit of $3.6 million. Today, FedEx is worth more than $57 billion. This is an interesting story, but we won't risk our hard-earned money by gambling.

TWO
Gambling versus Investing

Unfortunately, many people gamble in the stock market. It's not just average people; even seasoned professionals get sucked in, especially during good times. Picture a room full of men (Wall Street is still a male-dominated industry) wearing expensive suits, with advanced degrees, behaving strangely with other people's money. I read somewhere that it's hard to walk away from a winning streak, but even harder to leave the table when you're on a losing one. So, people keep playing until they run out of cash or max out their credit card(s). If you play long enough, the house always wins. This is why many investment companies go bankrupt during a recession—the wrong bets catch up to them.

I never gamble when I visit Las Vegas, but my dad loved to gamble at the local racetrack. Therefore, I know the difference between gambling and investing. How can anyone consistently predict which horse will win the race? There are so many factors to consider, such as weather, surface conditions, the horse's age, running style, previous injuries, the horse's demeanour before the race, its relationship with the jockey, the trainer's track record, and more. That said, my dad did win $100,000 in one race. It was a long shot that paid off, but as we all know, in the end, the house always wins if you keep playing long enough.

You have probably seen many gambling opportunities disguised as "can't lose" investment schemes. The probability of losing on a gamble always exceeds the probability of gain. In investing, the probability of a gain is expected to exceed the probability of a loss. Do your homework, look at the numbers, and think long-term. If you don't, then you are most likely gambling.

We had some experience investing in stocks, but that was our family's retirement accounts. It looked like a viable way to earn some passive income while we looked for other funding sources. I began doing some research and came across an interesting investment story. When Henry Ford decided to incorporate his fledgling auto business in 1903, he engaged Horace Rackham to draw up the required papers. Having no money to pay his lawyer, Ford convinced Rackham that an investment in the company might earn him his reward. In an uncharacteristic gamble, Rackham borrowed $5,000 and bought one hundred shares of Ford's stock. His bank manager advised him not to invest in Ford, saying "horses are here to stay!"

In 1908, the stock underwent a twenty-for-one split, and Rackham left the legal profession in 1913 to tend to his fortune. When Edsel Ford, acting as his father's agent, bought up all the Ford stock in 1919, Rackham's share was worth $12.5 million, with $2 million earned in dividends alone. The Rackhams lived modestly. They never flaunted their wealth, instead donating money to children's charities, the University of Michigan, and other causes.

Rackham prudently invested his wealth in municipal bonds, which survived the stock market crash of 1929. At the time of his death, his fortune was estimated to be worth $16.5 million. Perhaps investing in stocks was the way to go.

After conducting more research and consulting with members of our community and supporters, we decided Young Guns WC would become a social enterprise instead of a nonprofit. Our accountant agreed, and we established Young Guns Capital Corp. Social enterprises are businesses that sell goods and services with a social, cultural, or environmental purpose embedded into the business model, and reinvest the majority of profits into their social mission. Social enterprises sell all sorts of things; credit unions are an excellent example of this. A significant portion of the profits they generate from loans and banking fees goes toward funding various community programs and providing dividends to their members, who are also their customers. If you ever had a savings or chequing account at a credit union, you likely noticed the annual dividend payments automatically deposited into your account. It's a financial institution that deposits money into your account instead of always charging fees!

Another reason we decided to invest the money was that we learned that universities invest money in their endowment funds, and their returns over the years have been spectacular. Harvard University's endowment is valued at over $53 billion, making it the largest academic endowment in the world. With that much money, why do students need to take out student loans to attend Harvard? That's a topic for another day. Every day, the University of Texas System makes about $6 million off the land it manages in the United States's largest oil field. One year, Dartmouth College reported 47 percent returns, while the University of Pennsylvania posted 41 percent returns.

Many nonprofits invest surplus cash to generate income. If you are looking for a local example, check out your local community foundation. Community foundations are usually set up as nonprofit charitable organizations. They collect funds from donors/benefactors, invest the funds, and then use the income for the benefit of the citizens of the community in the fields of education, recreation, culture, and the humanities.

Local nonprofits and community groups can apply for grants, and some get approved. The foundations are typically made up of a group of volunteers who sit on the board and various committees. In our community, the Bursary & Scholarship Committee of the local community foundation handed out more than $104,500 in scholarships and bursaries to ninety-one local high school students in 2023. Funds are also regularly donated to local school district lunch programs. It is important that the foundation's funds are invested in securities with low fees, are diversified, and generate enough returns to cover their expenses.

Our community foundation's funds are currently invested in mutual funds, which I am not personally a fan of due to their high fees and typical underperformance compared to the broader market. However, looking through the foundation's past annual reports, I did notice that they directly held dividend-paying stocks many years ago, including:

- Canadian National Railway
- Suncor Energy
- Royal Bank of Canada
- Canadian Pacific Railway
- TELUS
- Shoppers Drug Mart Corp.
- Bank of Nova Scotia

Some of these stocks, such as Canadian National Railway (CNR), are also our favourites, and I will explain why in the book. Check out the CNR stock chart below.

Canadian National Railway

$152.92 ↑7,012.56% +150.77 Max

Aug 23, 5:40:00 PM UTC-4 · CAD · TSE · Disclaimer

| 5D | 1M | 6M | YTD | 1Y | 5Y | **MAX** |

CAD $2.19
Feb 7, 1997
Volume: 1.1M

Figure 5 - CN Rail stock trades on the Toronto Stock Exchange. It traded for around $3 a share in the late 1990s. Today it is over $150 a share. Source: Google Finance 2023.

I prefer dividend-paying companies because they deposit cash directly into shareholders' accounts. That is the joy of being a shareholder in a dividend-paying stock. Some companies' financial statements are difficult even for seasoned teams of accountants to understand. Depending on the financial metric you are looking at, a company could appear highly profitable, but have no cash flow. For example, a company may have 70 percent gross margins, but if customers regularly take six months to pay their bills, it will be difficult to meet payroll and cover regular expenses.

I have worked at a company where something similar happened. Some companies' expenses exceed their income, so they take on a lot of debt and then have trouble making it through difficult economic times. I have also seen some companies use debt to pay their quarterly dividends. This is not a smart long-term financial strategy, and it almost never ends well.

This made us feel more confident that investing our money was the way to go. We just needed to do serious research on investing in blue chip dividend stocks.

Investing is a personal endeavour. What we are about to discuss is our investing journey, which took place right in the middle of the COVID-19 pandemic. Albert Einstein said, "In the midst of every crisis, lies great opportunity." As we mentioned earlier, the pandemic restrictions shut down typical fundraising activities and many organizations stopped providing grants and funding. We saw investment opportunities in the market and decided to act. We hope this provides readers with some perspective. Everyone has different investment goals and risk tolerance.

There are many forms of exercise that may suit certain individuals. Some people are into powerlifting, yoga, running, boxing, golf, or pickleball, just to name a few. Some people switch activities as they age, or they just get bored. Investing is no different. I know many people who started out investing in mutual funds, switched to individual stocks, and now are in exchange-traded funds. Everyone's investment journey is different.

People can have a high-risk tolerance when they are making money, but it's a different story once the investments start underperforming. Most people don't have the stomach for investment losses. I felt that I had an obligation to share what I have learned in our journey and put it into a book. I hope readers find investing in blue chip dividend stocks less intimidating and feel comfortable with their investment decisions.

This book is intended for educational purposes only. The information provided here should not be considered investment advice. The information and statistical data included herein have been obtained from sources that I believe to be reliable. However, I cannot guarantee the accuracy of such information and accept no responsibility or liability for any errors, omissions, or inaccuracies. I strongly recommend that you seek expert professional advice before making any investment decision.

I have been investing in stocks since my early twenties, but the challenge now is to get my two teenage sons actively involved. Learning about investing, and personal finance in general, can be boring, especially for teenagers. So, I needed to find a way to explain investing in dividend-paying blue-chip stocks that would make the process both entertaining and educational for them. During the COVID-19 lockdowns, schools were closed, sports were cancelled, and restaurants were only offering takeout. Basically, our homes became a prison, and our family members became our cellmates. Just kidding. One night, while scrolling through Disney+, I got inspired to use superheroes to explain investments.

THREE
Lex Luthor Holds Assets. Superman Holds Debt.

During the pandemic, when we had to stay home and all sports were cancelled, we started streaming shows. One old TV show we watched was *Smallville*, on Amazon Prime Video. It's about Clark Kent's (Superman's) teenage years growing up in Smallville, Kansas. He is in high school and learning to deal with his super-powers. Clark's parents are farmers and struggle financially. They are always talking about debt and how they can qualify for a new loan, even though Clark does the work of at least five people on the farm. How can you be losing money if Superman is your employee? Something is seriously wrong with the business plan.

Lex Luthor's father is a billionaire with numerous businesses under his company LuthorCorp. He is always trying to explain to a young Lex the importance of growing their assets to expand the family empire. LuthorCorp is a publicly traded company, which is why Lex is always checking the stock price on his laptop. Their fertilizer plant in Smallville isn't profitable, so he sends Lex there to cut costs to make it profitable. A plant losing money is a liability, not an asset.

> "The rich hold assets. The rest hold debt."
>
> — Garth Turner, Turner Investments

The most important lesson you'll learn from the popular book *Rich Dad Poor Dad* is to seek to own more things that pay you each month and own fewer things that require a monthly payment from you.

Dividend-paying stocks are assets that pay you every three months; some even pay monthly. On the other hand, a new luxury car you bought using a massive loan is a liability that will cost you hundreds to thousands of dollars every month in payments, insurance, gas, and maintenance. Lex Luthor's fertilizer plant is an asset, whereas Superman's family farm is a liability.

The rich also don't leave large amounts of cash sitting in savings accounts. They invest and grow their money. The best way to do that is to take time to learn how to manage money and take calculated risks.

In Smallville, Lana Lang approached Lex Luthor about investing in her business idea. She wanted to convert an old movie theatre, which Lex had just purchased, into a popular coffee shop targeting youth, making it an entertainment venue featuring live music. It included a one-bedroom apartment upstairs. Lex made it clear that he would invest, but Lana would have to do all the work to make it viable, and he would get a large share of the profits. This again proves that Lex invests in assets.

Start small, like buying a few shares in companies you know. Some shares are as cheap as $1. You should know at a basic level how those companies make money because some companies don't. This is the best way to start learning how the stock market works. As we mentioned before, you will either make money in the beginning or you will learn some valuable lessons for next time.

FOUR
Invest in Companies That Spend Less than They Make

Most millionaires are like the X-Men: superhumans among regular people. In this section, we will discuss millionaires and how you can relate their habits to companies you may want to invest in.

> "These people cannot be millionaires! They don't dress like millionaires, they don't eat like millionaires, they don't act like millionaires—they don't even have millionaire names."
>
> —*The Millionaire Next Door*

The book *The Millionaire Next Door*, by Thomas J. Stanley and William D. Danko, was originally published in 1996 and became very popular. The book explains in detail that the popular concept of a millionaire is false, and most millionaires featured in the book live below their means. It also details that many high-income professionals, such as doctors, lawyers, and executives, are not wealthy. These people fail to accumulate any lasting wealth. They look rich and might feel rich, but they are not wealthy, just like some companies that you research and discover are not profitable and use debt to cover their day-to-day expenses.

A CEO of a major corporation once told many of his employees, "We have a lot of great art on the walls at our corporate offices. We don't buy art; we buy companies that bought too much art."

The Millionaire Next Door details how most millionaires live below their means and wear regular clothes while saving and investing their money. Many wealthy individuals do not live in upscale neighbourhoods, spend exorbitant amounts on watches, or drive new luxury cars. Instead, they budget and watch where they spend their money. They understand that a $100 watch tells the same time as a $5,000 one and believe that frugality is the key to building wealth.

The millionaires described in the book are focused on increasing their net worth, which is when their assets are greater than liabilities. As such, they avoid taking loans (liabilities) to buy things that may have little or no value in a few years. Most of them have lived in modest homes for decades and have no mortgages. They view a new car as a depreciating asset, one that decreases in value each year. For example, a brand-new, high-end Mercedes that costs $100,000 might only be worth $30,000 after five years.

However, many high-income/low-net-worth people have no idea how much they spend each month. The book details that they constantly need to convince others of their success, which often leads to their financial downfall.

In contrast, millionaires watch where they spend their money. They acquire assets that appreciate in value and don't try to show off by buying expensive houses, cars, and other luxury items. They don't care about what others think of them. Once you take the time to understand their mindset, there's nothing to fear.

When applying this to companies you want to invest in, it's important to note that some companies will have huge corporate offices, private jets and company retreats overseas. Sales are there but not profits because of large expenses. Many publicly listed companies do not pay dividends. Some reinvest in their businesses, such as Amazon and Alphabet Inc. (Google). However, many companies that pay dividends show that they are disciplined with their money and can be a good investment opportunity.

FIVE
Luke Cage's Bar, Coca-Cola, and Two Ways to Make Money off Stocks

Marvel's Luke Cage, featured on Netflix, not only possesses super-human strength and unbreakable skin, but was also a small business owner before becoming a full-time superhero. After being wrongly imprisoned for a crime, he did not commit, he invested his money in a dive bar in New York City. The bar wasn't anything special, but it helped pay the bills. Luke lived in a small apartment above the bar, and it became a regular hangout for Jessica Jones, a private investigator with superhuman strength. The two started dating, which had the potential to end very badly given that Jessica was one of Luke's best customers.

Who doesn't want to be their own boss someday? If you search a library, or Google, for entrepreneurship, you will be overwhelmed by the amount of information available on the topic. It is as endless as the ocean. You will drown in it. Profits are crucial, and in Luke Cage's case, he needed to pay minimum for his drinks and then sell them for as much as possible to ensure high profit margins. The problem was Jessica wasn't paying for her drinks—she drank like a fish. This hurt his profits.

You don't need to have a degree in business to be a successful entrepreneur, but you must have a basic understanding of accounting. Before starting any business or making an investment, an individual must understand the difference between an income statement and a balance sheet.

EBITDA is not the name of the exotic person you met last night at Starbucks; rather, it stands for Earnings Before Interest, Taxes, Depreciation, and Amortization. Investors and bankers use it to measure a company's profitability. Successful entrepreneurs pay close attention to their balance sheet, as they aim to grow their equity while also understanding the importance of cash flow. Cash flow can make or break a business and having to wait months to receive payment from customers, while bills pile up daily, can lead to severe premature aging for the business owner.

Imagine being a business owner without having to worry about customers, employees, competitors, suppliers, complicated tax reporting, sales, inventory, equipment, legal issues, banking, cash flow, landlords (or tenants), and government regulations. This takes it to a whole different level if you are in the bar/restaurant business. Mistakes there can make your customers sick and could shut down your business for good.

There is no work/life balance for an entrepreneur, and many do not have control over their lives or time. If you sell your product or service out of a physical location, such as a bar, then you must be at the place every day and on time. This is why it makes sense that Luke Cage lived above his bar. Successful small business owners rarely take sick days and often work seven days a week for many years to establish their business. This is the price of admission to the show.

Could simply buying and holding dividend-paying stocks for the long term be considered a legitimate business? Could it generate enough money to cover your annual personal expenses?

From the research I have done, the answer is yes, you can, and many people are doing it.

> **"Buy stocks the way you buy groceries,**
> **not the way you would buy perfume."**
> — Ben Graham, father of value investing

The quote explains that one should look for "sales" or "deals" and not be swayed by hype and marketing when buying stocks. Grocery shopping is done consistently, and shoppers are aware of prices. If you regularly drink Diet Coke and it happens to be 70 percent off this week, it's a good idea to buy in bulk and stock up. This is the smart financial thing to do.

Warren Buffett is arguably the greatest investor of our time, and he is a student of Ben Graham's investing style. He bought his first stock when he was eleven years old and is famous for buying quality companies on sale and holding them for long periods of time (think decades). It's worked for him, as he has made billions. His current net worth is over $100 billion. Dividend stocks, such as Coca-Cola, are a major reason Buffett has been so successful for so long.

The Coca-Cola Company is one of the world's largest beverage companies, with more than five hundred brands. It has twenty-one billion-dollar brands, including Diet Coke, Fanta, Sprite, Coca-Cola Zero, Powerade, Minute Maid, and Simply. I was surprised to learn that Fanta is a billion-dollar brand. Brazil is the largest consumer of Fanta in the world.

Warren Buffett bought about $1.3 billion of Coca-Cola shares in 1988, making it the largest position in his portfolio at the time. Coca-Cola stock price dropped because of the stock market crash, and many thought the company was finished growing. To outsiders, it seemed like a huge risk to invest in Coca-Cola, but Warren did his homework on the company.

Warren, like a true entrepreneur, saw a great opportunity to invest. Using basic accounting skills, he discovered that Coca-Cola was generating serious cash flow: a 60 percent gross profit margin, which was incredible. It was like Google today, but Google doesn't have any factories or delivery trucks. Coca-Cola's return on equity in 1988 was about 33 percent (the same now) when the average US corporations was about 12 percent.

Return on equity is one of the most important metrics for investors. It's a measure of overall profitability and of how well the company's leadership manages its shareholders' money. The higher the gross profit margin and return on equity numbers, the better.

Coca-Cola also had a strong brand name and the world's largest beverage distribution system. There were places on earth where you couldn't get clean drinking water, but you could buy a can of Coke. Warren knew this.

Looking at the numbers, it made perfect sense to buy Coca-Cola stock. Since 1988, the Coca-Cola dividend has increased by almost 1000 percent. In 2020, Coca-Cola paid Warren over $640 million in annual dividends. In 2022, Warren received $704 million in dividend income. That's a pay increase we all would love to have. Based on Coca-Cola's dividend history, the dividend will continue to grow. Warren's initial $1.3 billion investment is worth around $22 billion today. It still remains one of Warren's largest holdings today. Let that sink in for a minute.

There are two ways to make money off stocks: dividends and capital appreciation.

James Quincey, CEO of the Coca-Cola Co., earned approximately $23 million in 2022, making him the highest-paid employee at Coca-Cola. As the CEO, he worked tirelessly, travelling the world, making tough business decisions, and serving as the intermediary between seven hundred thousand employees, the largest institutional investors in finance, and millions of customers, including McDonald's (39,000 restaurants). If he were to make several significant business mistakes or lose market share to Pepsi, investors would quickly lose patience and demand a change. The company's board of directors would give in and replace the CEO. Even the CEO does not have job security.

Since 1988, Warren Buffett has basically done nothing but drink five cans of Coke a day. He has collected billions in annual dividends off Coca-Cola stock. That is the difference between an investor and a highly paid employee.

Let's use the Coca-Cola 1989 investment as an example of how a regular person can profit. After graduating from college and working for several years, you decide that you want to be your own boss. Like all young people, you think it would be a good idea to open a bar. It is the eighties, and that is where everyone hangs out after work. You manage to save up and borrow $130,000 from family and friends.

While conducting research, you learn that most bars fail before their fifth anniversary. It is scary to think that you would likely lose your entire investment in less than five years. This is why it's tough to get a bank loan to start one. As you look for suppliers, you discover that Coca-Cola or Pepsi are present in nearly every bar or restaurant in the world. Rum and Coke, vodka and Sprite, whiskey and club soda, etc. Coca-Cola brands are popular mixes at bars and restaurants. Even if you don't drink alcohol, any beverage someone is going to drink in a bar or restaurant will be either a Coca-Cola or Pepsi product. That's the power of marketing and branding.

Your research has also uncovered that Coca-Cola also owns Columbia Pictures. Yes, Coca-Cola is in the movie business, and it has produced some of your favourite movies, such as *Ghostbusters* and *The Karate Kid*. Additionally, they own popular and profitable TV shows, such as *Jeopardy!* and *Wheel of Fortune*.

Now you are really interested in investing. (Although in 1989, Coca-Cola sold Columbia to Sony Corporation.)

Check out Coca-Cola's long-term stock chart below.

Coca-Cola Co

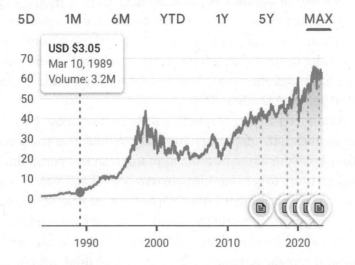

$60.27 ↑5,585.85% +59.21 Max

After Hours: $60.20 (↓0.12%) -0.070

Closed: Aug 23, 7:52:57 PM UTC-4 · USD · NYSE · Disclaimer

You changed your mind and decided to buy Coca-Cola shares with the entire $130,000 ($3.05 a share X 42,633 shares) in 1989. You decided to work full time as a bartender and pay off the loans. Fast forward to 2023, and the share price is now $60. The annual dividend has also grown significantly over the years. What does this mean for you, personally?

If you hadn't sold any shares, today you would be earning $78,445 a year in dividends. Coca-Cola's annual dividend is $1.84 X 42,633 shares. Just like Warren Buffet, you wouldn't have to do anything to get that dividend. You could play video games all day, every day, if you wanted to. Dividends are taxed much lower than salary income, so you would have kept most of the $78,445. That is equivalent to making over $100,000 a year working full-time (sixty hours a week at most jobs to get that income). Income taxes take a huge chunk of your gross pay. The total value of your Coca-Cola shares today would be worth over $2,557,980 million (based on a $60 share price). If you bought the shares in a tax-free or retirement account, then you could sell the shares and not pay any tax. If you had reinvested the dividends over the years and bought more shares, your dividend and total value would be much higher. We want to keep the math simple for this example and assume that you spent all your annual dividends when you got paid.

Coca-Cola has paid quarterly dividends since 1920 and has been increasing the dividend annually since 1963. 60 years of dividend growth.

Interesting information but how does this help regular people like you and me? In the middle of the Great Depression a banker in Quincy, Florida named Pat Munroe noticed that people were still buying bottles of Coca-Cola with whatever little money they had left. At the time, Coca-Cola shares were cheap based on various important financial metrics: bottom-line profits, cash balance and returns on equity were all high. Based on the numbers, it was a great investment. Munroe also realized nothing competed with its brand power. That is tougher to capture on a balance sheet, especially back then. You must pay attention to what people are doing and saying about the company. Investing is an art and a science.

Not only did Munroe invest in Coca-Cola shares himself, but he also urged many of his neighbors to do the same. He was a trusted banker, and many of them followed his advice. He'd even underwrite bank loans to widows and farmers backed by their Coca-Cola shares.

The farming town was able to keep afloat during the Depression with its Coca-Cola dividends. When the economy improved, Munroe and his town continued to buy shares of Coca-Cola. The share price continued to surge and by the late 1940s, Quincy, Florida (population approximately 4,000) became the richest town per capita in the entire United States. It is reported that the town had 67 Coca-Cola millionaires, and many of these early investors and their families still hold their shares today.

For you Pepsi lovers, look at the company's dividend growth rate since 1998, below, the year soda consumption in the United States peaked. PepsiCo has been paying dividends since 1965.

Pepsi annual dividend in 1998: $0.52 a share
Today: $5.06 a share

Another way to think about it is to look at PepsiCo's dividends over the years and imagine that was your paycheque. Has anyone's salary gone up ten times since 1998? PepsiCo's share price was hovering around $40 in 1998. Today, the share price is $182.

What happened to Luke Cage's bar? Kilgrave, a sociopath enhanced with a power of mind control, loved Jessica Jones but couldn't control her mind anymore. She was happy with Luke, and this angered Kilgrave. Kilgrave took control over Luke Cage's mind and ordered Cage to blow up his bar with himself in it. Luke survived, but the bar was destroyed, along with his home. This is an example of a business owner literally destroying his own business. Sometimes it makes sense to just invest in solid companies and collect your dividend cheques. It's much harder for your partner's ex to destroy that.

SIX
Why Buy Stocks that Pay Dividends?

"All the math you need in the stock market,
you get in the fourth grade."

— Peter Lynch, legendary investor

We chose not to invest in Coca-Cola. Yet. Instead, we bought shares of other publicly traded global companies that had a history of not only paying dividends, but also increasing over time. Can anyone buy shares of publicly traded companies? Yes, anyone who can open a basic brokerage account can invest in large global corporations, such as Starbucks, McDonald's, Nike, Suncor, and CN Rail. Look for companies that pay dividends and increase them consistently over time. Dividends are payments made by a company to its shareholders out of its profits (sales less expenses). They can be paid monthly or every three months and are important to long-term investors. Dividends provide a consistent and reliable stream of income to pay monthly bills, such as a cell phone bill. Many large companies increase their dividends every year to keep up with inflation.

"If money didn't grow on trees, then why do banks have branches?"

— Dad joke

The top five Canadian banks have been paying and increasing their dividends for more than 150 years. Yes, you heard that right. The Bank of Montreal is Canada's oldest bank, incorporated in 1817. It started paying dividends in 1829. It has been paying dividends to shareholders for more than 190 years, and it has not missed a single payment. Bank of Nova Scotia and TD Bank have all paid dividends for more than 160 years.

You can start using dividends to pay your recurring bills today. For example, let's say your monthly cell phone plan costs $75, or $900 annually. Many Canadian telecom companies, such as BCE (Bell), offer a dividend yield around 5 percent. To generate enough income to cover that bill, you would need to invest $18,000. By doing so, you can eliminate the need to pay your cell phone bill out of pocket, and in most cases, the share price of the company will appreciate over time. That's cool.

Railways are highly profitable businesses as they transport goods across North America and increase their prices annually. In Canada, customers do not have a choice because there are only two railway companies. CN Rail is one of the largest rail companies in North America. It has a strong history of raising quarterly dividends:

March 2, 2000: $0.03
March 10, 2023: $0.79

In 2000, CN Rail's share price was around $3, but today it has grown to $160. That's a significant increase!

Microsoft, founded in 1975, is one of the oldest technology companies in existence. They launched Windows 95 in 1995, and since then, they have dominated the office suite market with nearly 90 percent market share. Microsoft also owns popular products, such as Xbox, Minecraft, and LinkedIn. Their dividend history is also impressive:

January 16, 2003: $0.08
March 16, 2023: $0.68

In 2003, Microsoft's share price was around $25, but today it has grown to $279. Talk about compound growth.

Interestingly, Bill Gates and his family were the largest shareholders of CN Rail at one point. Today, Bill is the largest farmland owner in America, with over 250,000 acres of land in the United States. However, there's probably nothing to worry about. He's just one of the richest people on the planet buying up as much farmland as he can.

Another company to look at is Starbucks. Before delving into the financial details, let's read the remarks made by Howard Schultz, CEO of Starbucks, in the August 2010 issue of the *Harvard Business Review*:

> During the 2008 financial crisis people said that buying a latte at Starbucks wasn't smart. McDonald's put-up billboards saying that four dollars for a coffee is dumb. I have saved every analyst's report and major story (in 2008). My favorites were:
>
> * Never give an 800-pound gorilla caffeine
> * Starbucks' days are numbered
> * McDonald's will definitely kill Starbucks
> * How could the board bring back Schultz?

It costs Starbucks less than $1 to make lattes that sell for $6 to $7. According to their 2020 annual report, Starbucks has more than 30,600 coffee shops in sixty-three countries. On average,

Starbucks has over five hundred customers walking into their stores every day. Get in line to buy your pumpkin spice latte and focus on dividend increases. Starbucks' quarterly cash dividends are as follows:

April 23, 2010: $0.05
March 28, 2023: $0.53

Starbucks' share price was around $11 in 2010. Today it's around $100!

> "Investing is the only business where when things go on sale, everyone runs out of the store."
>
> — Some random guy on Twitter

It can be done in real life. Vermont-based janitor and gas station attendant Ronald Read died at age ninety-two in June 2014. Read had quietly amassed an $8 million fortune, thanks to smart spending and investing habits. "Mr. Read owned shares of at least 95 different companies at the time of his death, many of which he had held for years, if not decades," the *Wall Street Journal* reported in 2015. Some of his companies included Procter & Gamble, J.P. Morgan Chase, J.M. Smucker, CVS Health, and Johnson & Johnson. These are solid blue-chip companies that had a history of increasing their dividends. He left $6 million of his fortune to his local library and hospital. His donation had a serious measurable impact on his community. This example proves that anyone can do it.

This is why you buy solid companies that have a history of increasing their dividends. You make money two ways: dividends and capital appreciation.

SEVEN
Doctor Strange Should Have Invested in Stocks

Learning about investing in stocks can get boring, so let's use some superhero examples to help explain how it all works.

In the movie *Batman Begins*, a young Bruce Wayne left Gotham City and spent seven years travelling the world, training in combat, and hanging around criminals. He got involved with the League of Shadows criminal organization and burned down their temple. Afterward, he made a call, got on his private plane, and landed in Gotham City.

In *Ironman*, Tony Stark was captured and kept in a cave for three months. After escaping, he was seen in his private jet and driving in his Audi to a press conference.

Most people would lose their house and car if they didn't make any money for three months. Even doctors and lawyers must work to maintain their lifestyles. Look at what happened to Dr. Strange after his hands were crushed in a car accident and he couldn't work as a neurosurgeon. He quickly went from living the high life in New York City to being broke and then beaten by petty thieves in Nepal.

This brings me to one of Warren Buffett's famous quotes: "If you don't find a way to make money while you sleep, you will work until you die." What Warren, a mega-billionaire investor, is talking about is passive income.

Passive income is income that requires little to no effort to earn and maintain. You don't need to trade your time for money as you would with a part-time or full-time job. Dividend stocks are one of the simplest ways for investors to create passive income. Let me explain.

When you buy stock in a company, you are basically buying a small part, or share, of that company. Your ownership entitles you to a share of the company's profits and losses. In any business, it's the employees and managers that do the hard work of bringing in the sales and keeping costs under control. The board of directors and CEO look at the financials and decide every three months how much profit is returned to stockholders. This is called the dividend payment.

They do all the work. You, as the investor, are required to do nothing but collect your dividend and decide how to spend it.

Apple stock pays a dividend every three months. Apple started paying a dividend in 2012. Since then, Apple has more than doubled its dividend payment. The stock price has also gone up almost eight times (from $20 to $160). Investors who bought the stock were not required to do anything afterward. They stayed glued to their iPhone, scrolling their social media feeds, while the Apple stock price and dividends continued to rise.

Getting the latest iPhone with three cameras on a monthly payment plan will cost you money every month. You will probably need to upgrade your phone in two years, so more money will be spent. After five years, the phone will most likely be worthless. Life is all about choices. New Apple iPhone or buy Apple shares? You need to think long term and make the hard decisions.

Wayne Enterprises and Stark Industries kept paying Bruce Wayne and Tony Stark dividends. The money was regularly deposited into their bank accounts, and people like Alfred and

Penny made sure staff salaries and the bills were paid on time. Otherwise, there would have been nothing left when these two returned to their homes.

If Doctor Strange was so smart, he should have read some books on investing and learned the power of passive income.

EIGHT
Captain Marvel: Don't Invest Like It's 1995

Captain Marvel, one of the universe's most powerful heroes, is an alien warrior who finds herself caught in the middle of an intergalactic battle between two alien races. She keeps having recurring memories of another life as US Air Force pilot Carol Danvers.

The movie takes place in 1995. In one scene, Captain Marvel crash-lands through the roof of a Blockbuster Video store. If you need a refresher on Blockbuster Video, here it is. Back then, if you wanted to watch a movie, you had to drive to a movie store like Blockbuster and hope they had your movie on DVD or VHS. The popular movies were always rented out, especially on weekends. The movie rental was about $5, and you had to return it the next day. If it was late, you paid late fees.

At its peak in 2004, Blockbuster had sixty thousand employees and nine thousand stores worldwide, with a market value of $5.9 billion. Blockbuster is now bankrupt.

What happened to Blockbuster Video? It is the combination of a lot of things: The wrong people were hired to lead, the business environment changed, people no longer wanted their products or services, and technology changed. Terrible business decisions were made. The government decided to pass laws that affected their business. Threats to their organization became larger and eventually destroyed the company.

Back in September 2000, Blockbuster could have bought Netflix for $50 million, but the CEO of Blockbuster passed on the deal and couldn't stop laughing during the meeting.

Netflix was founded in 1997. It is worth $150 billion today and has over nine thousand employees. It made $32 billion in revenue in 2022. The Blockbuster executives don't look so smart now.

In 1995, the Internet was just getting started. Amazon's head office was a car garage in Seattle. Google and Facebook weren't invented yet. Apple was a well-known but small computer company. The computers in the nineties were massive, and you needed a large desk to store and use them. There were no iPhones or iPads, and only a few people had laptops. Most of the population didn't even have an email address.

It Is Better to Walk Alone than with a Crowd Going in the Wrong Direction

On September 14, 1995, General Electric (GE) crossed the $100 billion mark, becoming one of the most valuable companies in the world. It was an industrial conglomerate involved in jet engines, appliances, light bulbs, entertainment, financial services, energy, and health care. GE owned so many businesses that it was hard to keep track of them all. They even owned NBC and *Seinfeld*, a hugely popular nineties TV show that still airs today.

Jack Welch was the CEO of GE and was a management superstar. Fortune magazine called him "the manager of the century" in 1999, and at least twenty books were written about him and his leadership style at the time. If you were taking any university business class in the nineties, you knew about GE and Jack Welch.

In investing, if a high school student can't explain the business and how it makes money, then it's best to not to invest. General Electric became one of those companies. Global investment firms and multi-billion-dollar pension funds couldn't make sense of GE's complicated financials. Not a good sign. They began selling stock, and everyone else followed.

GE made big bets at the wrong time and began losing money. They first cut their dividend in 2008, and the stock price started to drop sharply: not a good trend. Companies that regularly cut dividends are not well-liked by investors, and this trend can cause a downward spiral.

According to *Forbes*, GE hit a $600 billion valuation in 2000. Over three hundred thousand employees worked at GE around the world. However, GE's downfall started in 2001, and today, it is worth $100 billion. That's a significant decrease in market value.

In contrast, the stock prices of Amazon, Google, Facebook, and Apple continue to rise dramatically. These companies now have a combined market cap of over $5 trillion dollars.

This is not new, as history has shown us that even the largest empires eventually fall, and new ones emerge. At one time, the British Empire was one of the largest empires in the world. The British ruled about 20 percent of the world's population from London and governed nearly 25 percent of the world's land-mass, including colonies such as the United States, Canada, Australia, India, Singapore, Hong Kong, large parts of Africa, and some areas of South America. Britain even corrupted an entire nation—China—with opium purely to extract drug revenues. Britain was truly a global superpower at the time.

Then, like all empires before it, it collapsed. The financial burden of two world wars eventually ended the British Empire. Colonies, such as India, were tired of dealing with racist policies that made its people second-class citizens in their own country, and they began to push for independence. After the Second World

War, Britain no longer had the wealth or strength to manage an empire overseas. The last significant British colony, Hong Kong, was returned to China in 1997.

China is now considered a global superpower in the economic, military, and technology fields. India is also emerging as a superpower.

Scotland is seriously considering leaving the United Kingdom, and England is now having a tough time just keeping its own country together. No one could have predicted this in the 1990s, yet here we are.

Success contains the seeds of its own destruction. It doesn't matter if it's Blockbuster, General Electric, or England. Companies and empires rise and fall, so it's not a good idea to put all your eggs in one basket. Apple is the most valuable company on Earth today, with a valuation of $3 trillion dollars, but it's still not wise to put all your money in Apple stock. Now you know why.

> "There's a world market for maybe five computers."
>
> — IBM President Thomas Watson, 1943

Even the best investment minds get it wrong or sell a stock too early. Legendary investor Warren Buffet purchased a 5 percent stake in Disney in 1966, which was worth $4 million. He quickly sold that stake for a 50 percent gain in 1967. If he had held onto the stock and reinvested all the dividends as they came in, the investment would have been worth more than $5 billion.

It's important to be diversified and buy many stocks and exchange-traded funds (which will be discussed in the next section). We prefer companies that have a long history of growing their dividends. Remember that some companies will exceed your wildest expectations, while some of the largest corporations can go bankrupt one day. No matter how smart you are, or the amount of research you have done on the company, there are simply too many variables out of your control. Here is an example from Volvo.

In the 1970s, North Korea ordered one thousand Volvo cars from Sweden. The cars were shipped and delivered, but North Korea just didn't bother paying and ignored the invoice. To this day, the bill remains unpaid, making it the largest car theft in history.

Not long ago, Marvel Entertainment's executive team, who are primarily middle-aged men, questioned the profitability of female-led superhero films, stating that "women can't carry a superhero movie." However, *Captain Marvel* proved them wrong as it was a major worldwide box-office success, generating over $1 billion dollars. This unexpected success may lead to more solo female superhero films being made in the future, representing a significant change in the entertainment industry.

NINE
Avengers, S&P 500 Index, and Exchange-Traded Funds

If a massive alien army invaded New York City, which Marvel hero would you pick to be on your team? Would it be Iron Man, Thor, Captain America, Hulk, or Hawkeye? What if you could pick the entire Avengers Team? That would be the best option.

Well, that's what investors do when they buy exchange-traded funds (ETF) instead of individual stocks. ETFs are pooled funds that bundle anywhere from one hundred to three thousand stocks together to offer investors a diversified portfolio. This is basically what mutual funds are, but ETFs trade throughout the day on exchanges like a stock, and you can see the price fluctuations in real time.

If there was a Superhero ETF (if stocks were superheroes), it would include Avengers, Spider-Man, Dr. Strange, Captain Marvel, Black Panther, Wolverine, Gambit, Daredevil, Deadpool, Luke Cage, and the rest of the Marvel superheroes. It doesn't stop there. You would also get heroes from the DC Comics universe: Batman, Superman, Wonder Woman, Aquaman, the Flash, and Green Lantern. You get them all on one team. How could you lose?

ETFs have become quite popular over the past decade because they have lower fees than mutual funds (more on this later) and are more diversified than buying a single stock. You saw in the earlier section how once-mighty corporations can fall and destroy shareholder value. Some ETFs pay dividends like regular stocks. The most popular ETFs closely track the S&P 500 Index.

The Standard & Poor's 500 Index is a market capitalization-weighted (how much a company is worth) index of the five hundred largest US publicly traded companies. It is one of the most followed indices by investors in the world because it is a benchmark for the entire US stock market. Every hotshot investor or money manager wants to beat the S&P 500 Index, yet almost all of them underperform, especially over the long term.

If the Superhero ETF resembled the S&P 500 Index, we would have all the superheroes because they are based in the United States, except for Wolverine (Canada), Black Panther (Wakanda), Wonder Woman (island nation of Themyscira), and Thor (Asgard). We will leave Superman (Krypton) in this group because he grew up in Smallville, Kansas. Not all superheroes could be included in the fund; only the biggest. *Jonah Hex* (2010 film played by Josh Brolin), *Steel* (1997 film played by Shaquille O'Neal), and *Howard the Duck* (1986 film) would not be included. If you don't remember these heroes or films, that's because they bombed big-time. Literally, no one went to see these movies.

Who Invented ETFs? How Did They Get Started?

Nathan Most was born on March 22, 1914, in Los Angeles, California. He was a physicist by training and worked as an engineer specializing in acoustics for the United States Navy during the Second World War. Later, he spent years travelling throughout Asia selling acoustic material to movie theatres. He eventually went into finance and started working for the Pacific Commodities Exchange.

During the 1980s and early 1990s, mutual fund sales were booming, but they couldn't be traded like stocks. Nathan Most saw an opportunity during the 1987 stock market crash when US markets fell more than 20 percent in a single day. He met with Jack Bogle, then head of the Vanguard Group. Most proposed using Vanguard's S&P 500 Index fund in a new structure, one that would enable investors to trade the index fund "all day long, in real time" like a stock.

Jack was not interested. Most was not discouraged and created the very first ETF listed in the United States: SPDR S&P 500 ETF (SPY). It began trading in 1993; the price was $45 a share and didn't pay a dividend. It tracked the S&P 500 Index. What was not anticipated was the interest in ETFs around the world. ETFs were starting to become a major rival to traditional mutual funds. Vanguard now has their own line of ETFs.

Today, SPY is the largest ETF in the world with $365 billion in assets. It recently traded over $400 ($45 in 1993). The annual dividend is currently under 2 percent. The fund has achieved average annual returns of 9 percent since 1993. Nine percent a year compounded for twenty-seven years really adds up. This fund has an expense ratio (fees) of just 0.09 percent. Most mutual funds charge between 2 and 3 percent and don't generate the returns mentioned above. Mutual funds employ many skilled finance/investment managers and staff who research and trade stocks. ETFs like SPY basically use a computer program to track the index. That's it. The fees on mutual funds can significantly reduce your investment returns. This can add up over time. In some cases, fees can add up to one-third of your total investment returns. A retirement portfolio of $500,000 would pay the following fees:

SPY $500,000 x 0.09% = $450 per year

US Equity or Index Mutual Fund $500,000 x 2% = $10,000 per year

You pay almost twenty-two times more in fees with this mutual fund versus the SPY ETF. With this one decision, a person can retire years if not a decade sooner. That is how much fees impact your returns over the long term.

You can now see why billions of dollars around the world continue to move out of mutual funds and into ETFs. Today, the global ETF industry has over $6 trillion of assets under management. In an ironic twist, Most never received a dime in royalties for the popular financial product he invented. He died in 2004, at the age of ninety.

There are now over 2,500 US-listed ETFs. There are even ETFs solely focused on video games, marijuana, and how to profit off North America's obesity problem. One ETF ticker symbol was SLIM, and it included stocks such as Weight Watchers, makers of plus-sized apparel, and pharmaceuticals specializing in weight loss supplements and diabetes treatment. You could now profit off your obese neighbour who only wears XXXL clothing, regularly eats at McDonald's, and needs expensive medications to manage his blood sugar levels. SLIM had great returns, generating 35 percent in 2018, easily beating the index. The parent company suddenly closed the fund in early 2020. They didn't provide any clarification. I think it was because of all the negative press they were getting. There is hope for humanity, and maybe for Wall Street. Maybe.

Companies in the S&P 500 Index change over time. In 2000, General Electric was not only the largest company in the S&P 500 Index, but also in the world. If General Electric stock was up for the year, then so was the S&P 500 Index. Today, General

Electric doesn't even rank in the top one hundred most valuable companies in the S&P 500 Index.

In 2008, Exxon Mobil was the largest corporation in the index. At that time, crude oil was trading at $147 a barrel (today it's $70), and Exxon made a record $45 billion in profit. Profit is calculated by subtracting expenses from sales, and $45 billion was what was left over after they paid for everything including tips. However, during the pandemic, the entire energy sector dropped to just 3 percent of the index. As fortunes can change rapidly, people prefer to buy index funds instead of individual stocks because diversification protects investments during a downturn in sectors or economies.

The year 2019 was a great year for S&P 500 Index investors; the index returned about 30 percent. This is why S&P 500 Index ETFs are popular, as they offer an annual return of 30 percent for buying an index with hardly any investment fees. However, almost all the gains came from technology stocks, such as Apple, Microsoft, Amazon, Netflix, Google, and Facebook. These stocks belong to a single sector of the economy. As of September 15, 2020, the technology sector hit a new high, making up 29 percent of the S&P 500 Index. Apple alone contributed 7.5 percent of the index, which is larger than several sectors, such as energy and materials. That said, technology companies are profitable. The following numbers are based on 2022 financials:

Profit Generated Each Hour:
Apple: $9.6 million per hour
Microsoft: $8.1 million per hour
Google: $6.9 million per hour
Facebook: $2.2 million per hour
Tesla: $1.5 million per hour
Amazon: $950,000 per hour

So much for diversification. When the technology stocks mentioned above perform well, the entire index performs well. But when these six stocks experience a drop, the entire index falls. That is what happened in 2022 when tech stocks fell more than 30 percent, causing the S&P 500 to end the year down nearly 20 percent. We had purchased Google shares, which were wildly profitable based on its search engine, but the stock price tanked. The markets are not always efficient or rational, so it's important to take advantage of the opportunities that arise.

If this were a US-based superhero ETF, then Superman, Ironman, Batman, Spider-Man, and Captain America would be responsible for most of the gains, even though there are hundreds of superheroes in the Marvel and DC universe.

In the world of technology, things move at a rapid pace; companies can rise or fall with each new product announcement. It's not like the toothpaste market, where Colgate-Palmolive has largely dominated for the past one hundred years. The next section will delve into the exciting business of toothpaste.

When you buy ETFs, it's like having almost all the superheroes on your side instead of relying on just one superhero. Anything can happen to one person, but the team helps each other out. In the first Avengers film, Iron Man lost power in his suit after directing the nuclear missile at the alien fleet. He was falling from the sky at a rapid speed and was sure to die on impact. It was Hulk who leaped up from a skyscraper and saved him. If the Avengers do go to war again with an invading alien army, it's probably best to sell your insurance stocks. You saw what happened to New York City the last time they went to battle.

TEN
Why Don't the Investment Bros Talk about Toothpaste?

So, with all this disruption, where can someone invest where new technology or innovation won't destroy the company overnight? According to our research, the answer is toothpaste, or oral care, if you really want to get technical.

Want a guaranteed 50 percent return on your money for the next two years? Buy toothpaste in bulk when it's on sale.

Have you ever seen *Charlie and the Chocolate Factory*? In the book and 2005 film adaptation, Charlie's father used to work in a toothpaste factory, screwing lids onto tubes, until he was replaced by a cheaper and more efficient machine.

The toothpaste business is quite interesting. There are only a handful of companies around the world that make toothpaste, even though it's a relatively simple business. Companies such as Colgate-Palmolive Company (Colgate) and Procter & Gamble (P&G) have been around for over a hundred years. Despite what happened to Charlie's dad's job, the toothpaste business in general has a low risk of technological disruption. It's unlikely that companies such as Tesla, Amazon, Google, or Apple will disrupt the industry anytime soon.

In the United States, Colgate had a 35 percent share of the toothpaste market in 2019. Crest and Oral B, divisions of P&G, had a combined market share of around 35 percent as well. They are always close.

They look like the Coca-Cola and Pepsi of the oral care market but the global market tells a different story. Colgate has a dominant position in the oral care market worldwide, encompassing toothpaste, toothbrushes, dental floss, and mouthwash. Colgate owns 41 percent of the global toothpaste market and 31 percent of toothbrush sales based on 2019 data, making them number one in both the toothpaste and toothbrush global markets. They are the second-largest player in the mouthwash market. All this information is publicly available in Colgate's Annual Report.

The world's population is close to eight billion people; almost half of them brush their teeth at least once a day, and some twice a day. This means that almost half of the world's population wakes up every morning and uses Colgate toothpaste. I can't think of a product or company that has that kind of reach. According to P&G's recent annual report, the Crest brand (including Oral-B) has the second-highest global market share, with nearly 20 percent. That is way behind Colgate, and other competitors are not even close. Let's look at the global numbers.

Colgate has been present in key emerging markets for a very long time. For example, the company entered Mexico in 1925, Brazil in 1927, and India in 1937. Colgate's toothpaste market share exceeds 80 percent in Mexico, 80 percent in Brazil, 30 percent in China, 30 percent in Russia, 50 percent in South Africa, and nearly 60 percent in Australia. It has more than a 50 percent market share in the oral care market in India. India's population is approaching 1.4 billion people. In terms of market share, Crest doesn't even show up in the top five in India.

Colgate's dominance in Latin America is incredible, considering "Colgate" means "go hang yourself" in Spanish. I would hate to have been the first person in charge of marketing or advertising when Colgate entered the Mexico market.

You don't have to be a dentist to understand that cavities continue to be a global problem that affects a large percentage of the world's population. Most dentists recommend brushing twice a day and flossing once a day, making Colgate a business with tremendous staying power and potential for future growth.

Colgate's gross profit margins are just over 60 percent (and have been increasing for years), comparable to those of Coca-Cola and Google. The higher the gross profit margin number, the better. The oral care business is very profitable. P&G's gross profit margin is less than 50 percent. Colgate wins again.

How did Colgate start? The young William Colgate left the family farm and started a small soap and candle business in New York City in 1806. Colgate entered the oral hygiene market in 1873, initially selling the toothpaste in glass jars. In 1896, Colgate became the first brand to sell toothpaste in a collapsible tube. Wow, talk about innovation. I am being sarcastic.

In 1955, Colgate lost its number-one ranking in the toothpaste market when its rival, Procter & Gamble Co., began selling Crest, the first toothpaste with fluoride. Colgate responded by adding MFP fluoride (sodium monofluorophosphate), an enamel strengthener and cavity reducer, to its toothpaste in 1968. Colgate Total, a line of toothpaste designed to protect against several conditions, including gingivitis, was introduced in 1997. That's about it! Since then, there has been no major technological breakthrough in almost twenty-six years, yet Colgate remains the number one brand globally.

Today, Colgate-Palmolive Company is a publicly traded consumer products company with $15.7 billion of worldwide net sales in 2019. Oral care is Colgate's largest segment, accounting for 46 percent of annual revenue. It is the world's largest maker of toothpaste.

In addition to its oral care line, the firm manufactures shampoos, shower gels, deodorants, and home care products that are distributed in more than two hundred countries worldwide (with international sales accounting for about 70 percent of its consolidated total). It sells popular soaps, deodorants, dishwashing liquids, and cleaners under powerful brands such as Palmolive, Speed Stick, and Ajax.

Colgate-Palmolive has been paying uninterrupted dividends on its common stock since 1895 and has increased payments for at least fifty-seven years. Talk about a business model that stood the test of time. Beautiful smiles are a profitable business. Currently, the dividend yields 2.5 percent annually, and with a payout ratio of approximately 52 percent, Colgate should have little difficulty continuing to make the payment. It's a cash flow machine.

University professors and the media don't like talking about companies like Colgate. They are too busy reporting on technology companies and what Elon Musk is doing. The real-life Iron Man is more exciting to talk about at parties than toothpaste. However, it's important to have so-called "boring" companies in your portfolio. They provide a firm foundation and help power returns over the long term.

ELEVEN
Teenage Mutant Ninja Turtles, Kids Investing, and Domino's Pizza

"Imagination is more important than knowledge.
For knowledge is limited, whereas imagination
embraces the entire world, stimulating progress,
giving birth to evolution."

— Albert Einstein

In 1983, struggling artists Kevin Eastman and Peter Laird were living outside Boston, Massachusetts. One night, as a joke, Eastman drew a turtle standing up, wearing a mask, with nunchucks strapped to its arms. Eastman wrote "Ninja Turtle" on the top of the page. Eastman proceeded to draw four turtles, each armed with a ninja-style weapon. Laird added "Teenage Mutant" to the "Ninja Turtles" title. At the time, they didn't think much of it.

They felt they were onto something, so in March 1984, Eastman and Laird created a new company, Mirage Studios (there was no actual studio, just Laird's living room). With a tax refund and some savings, they raised $2,000 and printed three thousand copies of their first comic book, *Teenage Mutant Ninja Turtles (TMNT)*. It was black and white, as color would have been too expensive. They used the leftover cash to run an ad in an industry publication. It worked. Comic distributors across the country started calling, and Mirage sold all three thousand copies within a few weeks. At the time, no one could have imagined just how big this was going to be.

For those of you who didn't grow up in the 1980s or 1990s, *TMNT* is about four superhero teenage mutant turtles named after Italian Renaissance artists. They were trained by their mutant rat sensei in the Japanese martial art of ninjutsu. They lived in the sewers of New York City and battled petty criminals, evil overlords, and mutated creatures, while attempting to remain hidden from society.

During the late 1980s and early 1990s, TMNT became an unstoppable global brand. Cartoon series, films, video games, toys, and other merchandise were hugely popular with kids. The *Teenage Mutant Ninja Turtles* movie was released on March 30, 1990. With a budget of $14 million, it made over $200 million worldwide and became a box office hit.

As a kid, I remember enjoying the TV show and going to watch the first movie when it was released. This was the first of six films in the series. The 2014 film, *Teenage Mutant Ninja Turtles*, earned $493 million, making it the highest-grossing film of the series.

The franchise has generated a total revenue of approximately $15 billion in merchandise sales since 1984. Two struggling artists fooling around with drawings in their living room created a multi-billion-dollar brand.

"People calculate too much and think too little."

— Charlie Munger

Charlie is a successful investor who many legends in the stock market look up to. He regularly points out that thinking is a surprisingly underrated activity in investing. When it comes to investing, financial figures are important, but they don't tell the whole story. You have to take time to understand other aspects of a business, such as the company's culture or the management's vision for the future. He is famously known for telling this story:

> There was this little boy in Texas. The teacher asked the class, "There are nine sheep in the pen, and one jumps out. How many are left?" Everybody got the answer right except the little boy, who said, "None of them are left."
>
> The teacher said, "You don't understand arithmetic."
>
> And the boy said, "No, teacher. You don't understand sheep."

Peter Lynch is one of the most successful and well-known investors of all time. He ran the Fidelity Magellan Fund for thirteen years. Between 1977 and 1990, Lynch averaged a 29.2 percent annual return, consistently more than double the S&P 500 stock market index, making it the best-performing mutual fund in the world. He retired in 1990 at the age of forty-six. His books, *One Up on Wall Street* and *Beating the Street* were national best sellers in the 1990s.

Lynch provides a detailed account of his analysis in the book *Beating the Street*. He mentions that you should never invest in any idea that cannot be illustrated with a crayon.

In 1990, a class of seventh graders in a suburb of Boston, Massachusetts, did a social studies project on stocks. The students had to do their own research and dig up stocks for a paper portfolio. Their teacher, Ms. Morrissey, began the first lesson by explaining, "Before my students can put any stock in the port-folio, they must explain exactly what the company does. If they can't tell the class the service it provides or the products it makes, then they aren't allowed to buy."

The students sent their stock picks to Lynch, who later invited them to a pizza dinner at the Fidelity executive dining room. The kids illustrated their portfolio with little drawings representing each stock. Lynch loved this because it illustrated the principle that you should only invest in what you understand. The kids' portfolio consisted of:

The Walt Disney Co.
Nike Inc.
Walmart
Pepsi*
McDonald's
Topps (baseball cards)
The Gap Inc.
IBM
Pentech International**

*In 1990, Pepsi owned Pizza Hut and Kentucky Fried Chicken
**Maker of coloured pens and markers

All companies made products that were easy to understand. There were no technology companies in the portfolio, except for IBM. The kids went for solid stocks with less debt and increasing profits. Not all their picks were successful, but that's the nature of investing.

The kids' portfolio returned a 70 percent gain over a two-year period (1990–1991), outperforming the S&P 500, which gained 26 percent in the same time frame.

Company 1990–1991 Gains

The Gap Inc.	320%
Nike Inc.	179%
Walmart	165%
Pepsi	64%
Walt Disney Co.	3.4%
IBM	3.6%

The students' stock picks outperformed 99 percent of all equity mutual funds at the time. These funds had managers who were paid considerable sums for their expert selections, while these kids were happy to get free pizza.

This example explains what Morgan Housel, popular personal finance writer and author of *The Psychology of Money*, often talks about:

> In what other field does someone with no education, no relevant experience, no resources, and no connections vastly outperform someone with the best education, the most relevant experiences, the best resources, and the best connections? This happens in investing.
>
> The first rule of compounding: Never interrupt it unnecessarily. The punchline of compounding is never that it's just big. It's always— no matter how many times you study it—so big that you can barely wrap your head around it. In 2004, Bill Gates criticized the new Gmail, wondering why anyone would need a gig of storage.

The kids' stock picks from 1990 have delivered mind-blowing returns over the past thirty years. In fact, most companies on this list have generated double digit annualized returns for at least forty years. Pepsi has delivered an annualized return of over 12 percent since 1926. Check out the increases in stock prices from December 23, 1990, to December 23, 2020:

Company	1990	2020
The Gap Inc.	$2	$20.43
Nike Inc.	$1	$141.60
Walmart	$8	$143.50
Pepsi	$13	$145.06
Walt Disney Co.	$8	$173.73
IBM	$28	$124.69

These are just stock prices. These companies have paid and increased dividend payments over time. There are two ways to make money off stocks: capital appreciation and dividends. Those dividend cheques really add up over the years. The total returns of these stocks over the past thirty years would be even higher if you reinvested the dividends and bought more stock. That's compounding at work.

Another company any seventh grader understands is Domino's Pizza. In 1960, while still in university, two brothers named Tom and James Monaghan borrowed $900 and bought a small Michigan pizzeria named Dominick's. The pizzeria was initially run by the two of them until James decided to sell his share for an old beat-up Volkswagen Beetle that the brothers used to deliver pizzas. James wanted to keep his full-time job at the US Post Office because the pizza business was too risky for him. James would later go on to work as a security guard. Tom purchased two more pizzerias and changed its name to Domino's Pizza. The Domino's logo has three dots, which represent the three original stores in 1965.

Tom realized early on that his restaurant would have to focus solely on delivery as he had limited dine-in capacity. This led to several innovations. Domino's pizza is credited with creating the first insulated pizza bags, which keep pizzas warm during delivery. Their biggest invention, however, was the corrugated pizza box, which is cheap, stackable, insulated, and remains sturdy despite the moisture and cheese from the pizza. This was a major advancement in pizza box technology. In addition, the pizza boxes provided space for advertising. The invention was so simple, yet brilliant. It has been almost sixty years since it was introduced, and it's still used around the world today.

There was no industry standard for pizza delivery times back then. Domino's Pizza had usually been making their deliveries in less than thirty minutes, so guaranteeing it seemed doable. Domino's created the thirty-minute guarantee in 1984 and to say that "thirty minutes or less" was a success would be a *huge* understatement. Not only did it significantly increase Domino's sales, but it also set the industry standard for delivery times, which still holds today. It was referenced in most TV shows and movies at the time, including *Teenage Mutant Ninja Turtles* (1990 film). In one scene, the Domino's delivery guy drops off the pizza, and Michelangelo shorts him three dollars, saying: "You're two minutes late, dude!"

Tom later sold Domino's to an investment firm for a billion dollars. Domino's expanded for decades, but the quality of the pizzas declined. Back in 2010, Domino's Pizza had a reputation for making terrible pizza. Customers shared comments such as, "Worst pizza I ever had" and "The crust tastes like cardboard." In response, Patrick Doyle, the CEO, appeared in TV ads and promised to "work days, nights, and weekends" to get better. Domino's Pizza stock was trading at $9 a share at the time.

Doyle's dedication to improving the quality of their pizzas and remapping the company's delivery systems with new technological solutions led to increased customer satisfaction. This, in turn, led to increased sales and profits. With the Domino's app, customers could check if their pizza was still in the oven or on its way. Also, they could even place an order by texting an emoji.

Just like in 1965, Domino's stores are optimized for delivery instead of dining in. Their store locations are selected based on the best delivery routes, not the most foot traffic. This is a huge savings on real estate costs. And because people typically order more than one pizza, the delivery expense tends to be a small percentage of the average order value. When was the last time you ordered only one pizza?

Domino's profit per restaurant is significantly higher than the average restaurant in markets dominated by third-party delivery players. Companies such as SkipTheDishes, DoorDash, and Uber Eats charge restaurants up to 30 percent in commission. Those restaurants' profits go to paying these companies for deliveries. Domino's, on the other hand, has a strong digital brand that has enabled them to deal directly with their customers without the need for a middleman that would cut into their profits. As a result, most restaurants are just keeping the lights on, while Domino's continues to thrive.

The savings get passed down to their customers. Domino's is roughly 30 percent cheaper than fast food in terms of feeding a family of four or getting a meal delivered from a casual dining chain. For a hungry family, you can't beat the value Domino's Pizza provides. We order pizza at least twice a week. It's cheap, easy, and convenient.

All this has led to sales and profits growing at double digits. Domino's U.S. and international retail sales have each grown by 10% compounded annually over the past 10 years. Domino's stock price today is over $386. It was under $10 a decade ago. The stock has risen by more than 4,000 percent since 2004, performing better than tech stocks, such as Apple, Google, Facebook, and

Amazon. Domino's has also built a brief track record of dividend hikes. It has raised its dividend every year since 2014.

Today, Domino's is the largest pizza chain in the world. According to their website, Domino's operates 18,800 stores in more than ninety countries around the world. Domino's had global retail sales of more than $17.5 billion in 2022, with over $8.7 billion in the United States and nearly $8.8 billion internationally.

Domino's sells an average of three million pizzas a day.

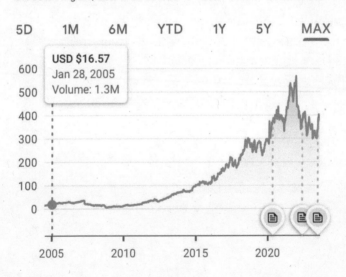

Figure 7 - During this time, it's interesting how Domino's outperformed all the mega technology companies. Sources: Statista, Yahoo! Finance (2020)

The Teenage Mutant Ninja Turtles loved pizza. In the 1990 movie version, the turtles would order pizza from Domino's and get it delivered around New York City, close to the sewers. The delivery driver would never see them. They were ninjas, after all.

TWELVE
Nicolas Cage, Walmart, and Buying Real Estate for Less than $300.

"You can print money, manufacture diamonds, and people
are a dime a dozen, but they'll always need land. It's the
one thing they're not making any more of."

— Lex Luthor, *Superman Returns*

Lex Luthor, the archenemy of Superman, always had a thing
for real estate. In the 2006 film, Lex's plan was to destroy the
United States, replace it with a large continent, and force the
rest of the world to live there. In the 1978 Superman movie, Lex
put a nuclear warhead on the San Andreas fault to cause a huge
earthquake that would have dropped California into the sea. This
would have greatly increased the value of his recently purchased
Nevada desert property. Beachfront property is always expensive.
In *Superman II*, Lex wanted Australia. This guy thought big in
terms of real estate investing, but it's a good thing for humanity
he failed every time.

Nicolas Cage was a top movie star in the 1990s and early 2000s. He starred in action blockbusters such as *The Rock, Con Air, Face/Off, National Treasure,* and *Ghost Rider.* He was one of the highest paid actors at the time. He won an Oscar and was considered to play Superman in an upcoming movie.

Cage was a spender, not a saver. The one-time Hollywood leading man spent millions on fifteen luxurious real estate properties around the world, including apartments on New York's Fifth Avenue, three castles (including an ancient Bavarian castle in Germany), a home in Beverly Hills, a townhouse in England, two islands in the Bahamas, and a haunted house in New Orleans. (How does a house of a former serial killer come into a real estate portfolio?) He also spent his fortune on exotic cars (including nine Rolls Royces), four yachts, and weird items such as a dinosaur skull that cost $300,000.

Back in 2007, everyone was buying real estate. Then the global financial crisis hit, and real estate prices crashed. Cage was in serious debt and had cash flow problems. He didn't make loan payments and stopped paying taxes. Cage ultimately declared bankruptcy in 2009. Strange, because according to Forbes magazine, he made $40 million that year. Perfect example of cash flow issues.

Never spend more than you make. Cage bought at the top of the real estate market and was forced to sell at the bottom. This is how most people lose money in real estate investing.

Arnold Schwarzenegger, on the other hand, became a multi-millionaire from investing in real estate in his twenties. Most people don't know this, but in the early 1970s, Arnold arrived in California and didn't want to rent an apartment. He had money saved up from bodybuilding competitions and decided to use it as a down payment to buy a six-unit apartment building. He wanted an income-producing property so he could train and go to school full time (he has a degree in business administration).

He lived rent free in apartment number six and rented out the other five units.

> "I put down money for an apartment building. I realized in the 70s that the inflation rate was very high and therefore an investment like that is unbeatable. Buildings that I would buy for $500K within the year were $800K and I put only maybe $100K down, so you made 300% on your money. I quickly developed and traded up my buildings and bought more apartment and office buildings."
>
> — Arnold Schwarzenegger

Since Arnold was rich, he was able to choose his film roles instead of taking any role that came his way. This is rare; most actors struggle with money and will take any role to pay their bills. Arnold didn't become a Hollywood action star until his thirties. The rest is history. Today his net worth is about $450 million.

The Terminator grew up dirt poor in a house that didn't have hot water or electricity, while Nicolas Cage grew up in a wealthy Hollywood family that included famous actors, producers, and the legendary Hollywood director Francis Ford Coppola, who directed the *Godfather* movies. Nicolas Cage's last name is actually Coppola, but he chose the last name Cage as a tribute to the comic-book superhero Luke Cage. Remember him? Cage attended Beverly Hills High School but dropped out to pursue an acting career in films.

> "Formal education will make you a living. Self-education will make you a fortune."
>
> — Jim Rohn, American businessman, a self-made millionaire before he turned thirty-one

Unlike day traders, successful real estate investors are long-term oriented, focused on income, and they wait patiently for appreciation. To be successful, you must be aware of what is happening in the economy. Arnold Schwarzenegger is a perfect example of this. Nicolas Cage is not.

Interest rates have been dropping since the 1980s, which has been great for real estate investors. In 1981, mortgage rates peaked at more than 20 percent. By 1990, they dropped to about 12 percent. Today, somebody can get a mortgage for about 5 percent. Low interest rates are important for real estate investors as they keep the bank loans and mortgage payments low. Generally, the lower the interest rates go, the higher the real estate prices spike. Successful real estate investors pay attention to interest rates.

Smart real estate investors, like Arnold, also pay attention to inflation. In the 1970s and 1980s, the rate of inflation averaged just under 10 percent, but since 1992, the inflation rate has generally stayed around 2 percent. If the inflation rate rises, then the Bank of Canada could start raising interest rates to bring it down.

Low inflation is important to people because it has a substantial impact on prices for the things we buy. Imagine if the price of a Big Mac went up by a dollar every year. People would not be happy. Real estate investors, however, would be happy because the value of their buildings would go up every year, making them wealthy like Arnold. Inflation numbers also help determine how much to increase the rent by every year. They will lose money if inflation hits 10 percent, while they only increase rent on their properties by 2 percent.

Would you like to own property? A second house? Maybe a small strip mall or commercial building? There are a lot of terms you need to know in addition to interest rates and inflation. You would need to know what leverage, triple net, capitalization rate (cap rate), net operating income, CapEx, appreciation, equity, debt-to-equity, mortgage, MLS, and cash flow are. When buying commercial property, it's important to know what the cap rate is. The cap rate indicates the rate of return that is expected to be generated on an investment property. The ideal cap rate is between 5-10 percent. The number will depend on the property type and location. Generally, lower than 5 percent means less risk. I have seen a McDonald's property for sale with a cap rate of around 3 percent.

People can lose everything with real estate investing since it requires so much capital and leverage. Leverage, in real estate, is using borrowed money to buy a property. The use of leverage in real estate investing amplifies both profits and losses, and, thus, increases risk, as well as expected return.

With leverage, you put 10 percent of your money down on a property and borrow the other 90 percent from the bank. This is how Arnold made a fortune in real estate when California property values were going up 20 to 30 percent a year in the 1970s. Nicolas Cage's Bel Air, California mansion was worth $35 million just before the real estate crash. It had a total of $18 million in loans. Due to unpaid loans, the bank sold the house to a new owner for $10.5 million in 2010. Remember, Cage had fifteen properties and most of them had loans on them. It unravelled fast. Leverage can make or break you.

There are people like Garth Turner, an investment advisor—who has also made money off real estate—who regularly brings up the harsh truth about real estate investing:

> You need diversification. Real estate is like every other asset class, prone to fluctuations. If you put all your net worth into one property at one location in one city, you're courting risk. That could be from macroeconomic events (a recession, rising interest rates) to the micro (the guy next

door starts a meth lab or the city approves a cell tower across the street).

Consider how to best weather some kind of economic storm. Houses (investment properties) become illiquid fast. Financial assets, in contrast, can be liquidated in seconds, giving you instant cash. Investment portfolios don't need to be insured, but real estate does. There are no property taxes, closing costs when you buy, or fat commissions when you sell. No maintenance. No grass cutting.

What if you could invest in real estate the same way you invest in dividend-paying stocks? The main objective of this section is not to argue with the HGTV viewers (where nobody ever loses money in real estate) or family members who are realtors. We are here to discuss how to get into real estate investing for under $300. So, we will focus on blue-chip stocks with significant real estate exposure and real estate investment trusts.

You need to watch *The Founder* on Netflix. Ray Kroc, responsible for McDonald's growth, has famously said, "They're in the real estate business, not the hamburger business." He was deep in debt, despite McDonald's early success, when he realized that "You don't build an empire off a 1.4 percent cut of a fifteen-cent hamburger. You build it by owning the land upon which the burger is cooked." Former McDonald's CFO, Harry J. Sonneborn, is even quoted saying, "we are not technically in the food business. We are in the real estate business. The only reason we sell fifteen-cent hamburgers is because they are the greatest producer of revenue, from which our tenants can pay us our rent."

McDonald's owns the land and buildings at most of its locations. The franchisees pay rent. This gives McDonald's more control over its franchisees and provides an even more stable revenue than franchise fees. You must always pay the full rent, even if sales are down. The banks love lending you money if you have real estate assets, so there is no limit to growth.

Today, McDonald's has over $30 billion in real estate holdings, making it one of the largest commercial real estate owners in the world.

McDonald's is one of largest fast-food chains. According to McDonald's Corporate, it has more than 38,000 franchise locations around the world. The company operates in 120 countries and opens an average of six hundred new locations each year. Due to their strong focus on real estate, the company generated $7.5 billion of rental income in 2019, which accounted for slightly more than one-third of its total corporate revenue of $21 billion.

McDonald's Stock Info

Share Price
2005: $33   2023: $278

Annual Dividend Per Share
2005: $0.67   2023: $6.08

McDonald's has raised its annual dividend for forty-seven consecutive years since paying its first dividend in 1976.

Walmart is another retailer that prefers to own its real estate. On July 2, 1962, Sam Walton opened the first Walmart store in Rogers, Arkansas. Walton's strategy was to dramatically cut prices on all products (reducing profit margins) to get customers into his store, which would then lead to higher sales and profits. People buy a lot of products when they are on sale. In the early days, Walmarts were initially located in small towns, instead of large cities where the established competitors operated. Walmart grew fast and competitors didn't notice until it was too late.

In 1985, Forbes magazine pronounced Sam Walton to be the richest man in America, with an estimated worth of $2.8 billion. Despite his wealth, Walton was famously frugal and continued to drive a 1979 Ford F-150 pickup truck. The steering wheel was chewed up by his dog. Today, according to Bloomberg, the Walton family is one of the wealthiest families in the world, with a combined fortune of more than $200 billion.

Walmart is one of the most successful and profitable retailers in the world. Walmart's 2020 total revenue was $559 billion. The company has over 11,400 store locations around the world. The average Walmart generates approximately $1 million a week in sales. Their competition doesn't even come close.

How did Walmart get into owning real estate when most retailers prefer to lease? Sam Walton was a highly successful retailer before he opened his first Walmart, but he was burned on a lease on his very first store because he didn't read the fine print. He neglected to add a clause in his lease that would give him the option to renew the lease. Walton's store was profitable, but the landlord refused to renew Walton's lease. The landlord took over Walton's store and transferred it to his son. The Walton family was devastated. This experience led the company to greatly prefer owning rather than leasing. Today, Walmart owns 85 percent of the real estate of its US stores and distribution facilities, as well as more than 50 percent of its international stores and distribution facilities. Additionally, Walmart's real estate division rents out store space at supercentres to McDonald's, banks, and other small businesses, and it also finds new uses for former Walmart stores.

According to Walmart's website, 90 percent of Americans live within ten miles of a Walmart store. Almost forty million people shop at Walmart every day (2019). Location! Location! Location! This is one of the reasons Walmart has been able to weather the Amazon online sales storm when many traditional retailers, such as Kmart, JC Penny, and Sears, have declared bankruptcy. If you don't want to wait three days for your video games to arrive from Amazon, just drive five minutes to the nearest Walmart and buy it ASAP.

Walmart Stock Info

Share Price
2005: $45   2023: $146

Annual Dividend Per Share
2005: $0.52   2023: $2.28

*Walmart has increased their annual dividend every year since first declaring an annual dividend in March 1974.

Real Estate Investment Trusts

If you don't want to own stocks and want pure play real estate companies, then you should look into investing in Real Estate Investment Trusts.

Real Estate Investment Trusts (REIT) are diversified portfolios of income-producing properties. Some REITs specialize in apartments, storage facilities, or even shopping malls. According to *Forbes*, REITs are basically "pass-through" investments: Management collects the rent, keeps enough money to pay for maintenance—possibly expansion and to keep the lights on—then hands the rest to shareholders as dividends. Some can provide capital gains.

A REIT trades similarly to exchange-traded funds or stocks. Unlike your house or the strip mall you own, you can see the value of your investment fluctuate in real time. For ultimate diversification, you can buy REIT exchange-traded funds (ETFs).

The Vanguard REIT ETF, which invested in about 145 different REITs, recently had an overall dividend yield of 4.1 percent.

The Vanguard REIT ETF has averaged 8.4 percent annually over the past decade, outpacing the S&P 500's 7.8 percent.

XRE is a Canadian REIT ETF. XRE provides exposure to approximately sixteen REITs across several subsectors in Canada. It has a dividend yield of 5.7 percent. Its average annual return is just over 10 percent a year. A management expense ratio of 0.61 percent a year is pretty decent. Most real estate mutual funds charge about 2.5 percent in management fees.

In *Superman Returns*, Lex Luther was already extremely wealthy after his ultra-rich elderly wife passed away, leaving her fortune to him. He was sailing around in a $100 million yacht that had a helicopter pad. He should have given up on his insane real estate plans for global domination and just invested in real estate stocks and REITs. He could have enjoyed the rest of his life making money off dividends and capital appreciation. Instead, he took on Superman, who is literally an alien god, and lost. Nicolas Cage is a huge Superman fan; he even named his son Kal-El (Superman's birth name). Come to think of it, maybe Cage should have played Lex Luthor in the movie.

THIRTEEN
Black Panther, Wakanda, Oil, Saudi Arabia, and Commodity Stocks

In the *Black Panther* movie, vibranium is a rare material found in the small African nation of Wakanda. Vibranium's unique properties allow it to absorb, store, and release large amounts of kinetic energy, making it nearly indestructible.

Black Panther's entire suit is made from a vibranium weave that's impossible to pierce because it robs objects heading his way of their momentum, including bullets. This also allows Black Panther to survive large falls when landing on his feet. Captain America's shield is also made from the same material, which makes it such an effective weapon and defence.

According to Marvel Comics, Black Panther, also known as King T'Challa, used profits made from selling small pieces of vibranium to turn Wakanda into the most technologically advanced country in the world. It powered almost everything in their country, including their technology and weapons. As king of the nation, he became even wealthier than Tony Stark.

A real-life example I can think of that would compare vibranium and its impact on the country of Wakanda would be the

Kingdom of Saudi Arabia (Saudi Arabia) and how it was transformed by the discovery of oil.

Let's start with a brief history lesson. Saudi Arabia was formally founded in 1932, when many regions were united into a single state, which followed a series of battles over the course of three decades. Ninety-five percent of Saudi Arabia is a desert, so not much grew there, and it was difficult to travel across the country. At the time, its citizens were generally poor, illiterate, and made a living off their livestock or by running small shops. However, in 1938, an American geologist discovered oil, which was eventually revealed to be the largest source of crude oil in the world.

With global demand for oil quickly soaring after the Second World War, Saudi Arabia began building an extensive network of roads, airfields, pipelines, and deep-water ports to accommodate the rapidly increasing flow of oil. Things were going well. Saudi Arabia was making billions of dollars off their oil but needed to develop their country. They wanted to transform from a medieval society into a modern, industrialized economy by building cities in the desert. As a result, Saudi Arabia became one of the fastest-growing economies in the world.

Today, oil is the most traded commodity in the world, and it touches almost every sector of the global economy. It is a major source of energy and a key component in the production of textiles, fertilizers, plastics, cosmetics, and even steel.

Did you know that comfortable, breathable, and lightweight clothes that allow you to bend and stretch every which way are made from petroleum? Yoga pants and, in general, much of the active wear we use when running and training is made up of a unique combination of spandex (a.k.a. Lycra) and nylon, both of which are derivatives of petrochemicals.

The global economy needs cheap oil. Oil prices generally rise during boom periods—as more oil is needed to manufacture and transport products—and fall during economic slowdowns.

The world pays close attention to oil prices and what Saudi Arabia does because Saudi Arabia can impact the price of oil by producing too much or too little. Oil now accounts for 90 percent of the country's exports and nearly 75 percent of government revenue. It would be the understatement of the century to say Saudi Arabia's fortunes are tied to the price of oil. If the price of oil drops, the country suffers. So far, the Saudi Arabian economy has continued to defy gravity and grow at a rapid pace.

GDP of Saudi Arabia:
1990: $117 billion
2000: $189 billion
2010: $528 billion
2020: $680 billion
2022: $1 trillion

Oil royalty payments enabled the Saudi royal family, the world's wealthiest, to enjoy an opulent lifestyle, including furniture and cars made of gold. They have also improved the lives of their people through major infrastructure and public works projects, such as the construction of schools and hospitals. Education and health care are free for its citizens, and many Saudi students attend universities in the United States and Europe. Also, citizens are not required to pay income taxes, which is a huge benefit. In Canada, for example, someone earning $100,000 a year can expect to pay over 40 percent in provincial and federal income taxes.

Saudi Aramco is primarily state owned and is the world's biggest oil producer, currently valued at $2 trillion. Only Microsoft and Apple are worth more. It has an estimated 270 billion barrels in reserves. The oil company pays a hefty tax rate of 50 percent to the Saudi Arabian government.

How did Saudi Aramco become one of the most profitable companies in the world? To start, the cost of conventional oil in Saudi Arabia is well under $10 per barrel, including transportation costs (The cost is similar to Iran and Iraq, but these countries have to deal with US sanctions and ISIS). Worldwide costs range from $35 to $50 a barrel.

A lot of this is due to basic geology. It's easy to extract oil from the Saudi desert because there are no rivers, lakes, or large areas of natural vegetation, due to scant or nonexistent rainfall. There are virtually no trees, and the dessert doesn't support much wildlife. The oil tends to sit in immense, highly concentrated pools close to the surface, making it easy to extract with just a good shovel. Many Saudi oil fields have been in production for decades, and there's still plenty of oil left. They keep pumping oil without any added costs. Additionally, they have an established network of pipelines that make it cheaper to transport oil to its seaports and then internationally.

This is why Saudi Arabia is a low-cost producer. If the oil market was retail, Saudi Arabia would be Costco.

What would Canada be then? Canada's population is about the same size as Saudi Arabia's—both have just under forty million people. Canada is the fourth largest producer of crude oil in the world, but extracting oil in Canada is a complicated process. Most of Canada's oil comes from northern Alberta, British Columbia, and Saskatchewan, which are covered with trees, rivers, lakes, wildlife, and numerous cities. This is why oil companies must comply with strict environmental conditions. This is a good thing. The lack of transportation infrastructure, such as pipelines to port cities, poses a major problem because Canada primarily sells its oil to one buyer, who sets the price: the United States. The cost of natural gas used to produce steam to extract the heavy oil, which is deep in the ground, and other operating costs are much higher than in Saudi Arabia. Much higher. In fact, eastern Canada imports billions of dollars' worth of oil every year from Saudi Arabia because it's cheaper than shipping it from western Canada.

The problem with the cyclical nature of commodities such as oil is that the boom periods tend to attract all kinds of investors, especially gamblers who become enchanted with the size of the short-term profits. Some of the companies even begin paying dividends and increasing them. This is what happened around 2008, and then again in 2014, as commodities like oil had a huge increase in prices. China was building mega cities and factories at every corner. They were buying up commodities, such as oil, coal, zinc, copper, gold, and uranium, at any price. India was also growing, and demand for commodities was high.

Many people started gambling with penny mining and oil stocks. Investment decisions were not based on financials but hope and hype. Then commodity prices started to fall as a global recession hit. Most investors lost all their investments. Many companies went bankrupt. The price of oil has been dropping since 2014, as anyone in Alberta can attest.

This is why commodity stocks are meant to be traded, not held for the long term.

If you look at twenty-year stock charts of almost all commodity stocks, such as Teck Resources (copper, zinc, and coal), Exxon Mobil (oil), Barrick Gold (gold), Canfor Corp. (lumber), and Cameco (uranium), you will notice that the share prices of these companies haven't moved much since 2000. They did rise and fall dramatically with the price of commodities during that time. Some traders have made fortunes by buying when commodity prices and stocks were at record lows and selling when the business cycle was at the top, but most have lost money. You can't time markets.

Suncor Energy

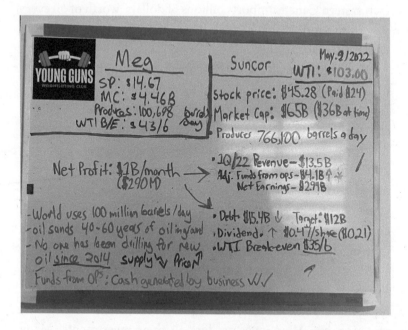

Figure 8 - We did an analysis of Suncor Energy before we decided to buy. Suncor makes money if the price of oil is over $35 per barrel.

Young Guns decided to invest in Suncor Energy (SU:TSX) as our first stock. How is investing in Petro-Canada gas stations going to help a free youth weightlifting club? Will this be sustainable? Oil prices generally rise during boom periods, as more oil is needed to manufacture and transport products, and prices fall during economic slowdowns.

At the time we invested, everyone was stuck at home because of COVID-19 restrictions, but that wasn't going to last. Eventually, the restrictions would ease, and people would begin driving and travelling more, which in turn would increase gas prices at the pump.

We researched many companies and decided to invest in Suncor Energy because it is Canada's largest integrated energy company, with four large refineries and roughly 1,500 Petro-Canada retail locations. It was worth more than $36 billion at that time (August 2021). This is not a penny stock. Owning refineries and pipelines is a major advantage for Suncor. When oil prices fall, for example, refinery margins often rise. We saw a few Suncor refineries in Edmonton, Alberta, and they looked like mini cities. However, 98 percent of oil companies do not have their own refineries and gas stations, so their profits disappear when the price of oil drops.

Back in early 2021, Suncor stock was trading at around $24 a share. The share price was at $45 before COVID-19 hit in January 2020. You have to buy them when nobody wants them, and the price of oil is rising. Some might say the markets are efficient, and stocks are not mispriced. Our thoughts are that stocks are still mainly bought and sold by people. The computers haven't completely taken over yet. People are not rational or efficient. Just sit in a traffic jam in any major city or attend a Black Friday sale and see what happens.

Suncor's breakeven price is around $35 for each barrel (WTI crude). With WTI trading at around $69 per barrel at the time, Suncor was making a lot of money, but the stock price did not increase. In fact, I remember that at the time, many in the investment industry were avoiding Canadian oil and gas stocks, and the stock prices crashed once the pandemic began. At one point, the price of oil went negative, and companies paid you to take their oil. You just had to figure out where to store it.

The price of oil did rebound, however, and companies such as Suncor started making profits again. When we decided to invest in Suncor in 2021, it generated a net profit of $868 million in the quarter. That's about $290 million in profit a month. The numbers made sense.

Suncor was using its profits to pay down debt and buy back shares. They felt their share price was too cheap to ignore. This was a smart financial move. The dividend yield at the time was 3.5 percent based on a $25 share price. We expected the dividend to rise over the next few years. If we were correct, the share price should follow. Today, the share price is $45, and the dividend is 5% (Based on current stock price). Suncor Energy has more than doubled its quarterly dividend since we purchased the stock.

Figure 9 – We decided to check on our investment in Edmonton, Alberta. This refinery is larger than most Canadian towns.

FOURTEEN
Nike: Buy the shoes
or the stock?

Have you seen the TV show *The Flash*? Barry Allen is a crime scene investigator with the Central City Police Department. Barry has a stable, well-paying job with a pension. Then, one day, he is struck by lightning during a freak storm and falls into a coma. Months later, he awakens with the power of super speed (about 700 mph), which he uses to fight criminals, including others who have also gained superhuman abilities. He becomes the Flash. The Flash is one of DC Comics' most popular characters. On several occasions, the Flash has raced against Superman; these races often result in ties.

Who is actually the fastest man in the world? That title belongs to Jamaican Usain Bolt. Bolt bagged a total of eight Olympic gold medals and numerous world championship gold medals throughout his career. He holds world records in the 100-metre and 200-metre distances, winning three consecutive gold medals and dominating the 2008, 2012, and 2016 Olympics. Everyone wants to know who the fastest man in the world is, and that is why he is so popular. Bolt is the greatest sprinter of all time.

If I were Barry, I would have joined the US Olympic team as a sprinter. The police job is stable, but sprinters can make a lot of money. As of 2020, Usain Bolt's net worth is estimated to be $90 million, making him one of the highest-paid Olympians of all time. Despite being retired, he still makes serious money off endorsement deals. One of his biggest endorsements is from Puma, which pays him $10 million annually.

Speaking of running shoes, do you know who Phil Knight is?

Knight was a middle-distance runner at the University of Oregon in the late 1950s. During his Master of Business Administration program at Stanford University, he wrote a research paper on why shoes should be manufactured in Japan (instead of Germany), where the labour costs were cheaper, but quality remained high. He went on to become a certified public accountant and worked at PricewaterhouseCoopers, one of the largest accounting firms in the world. He even worked as an accounting professor at Portland State University.

While working full time, Knight kept thinking about his research paper and his travels around the world. When he visited Japan, he met with company executives who produced Tiger sneakers. Tiger shoes were very popular in Japan, but nobody had heard of them in the United States.

In 1962, he decided to launch Blue Ribbon Sports, and began importing Tiger running shoes from Japan. Knight had no money in the beginning and had to borrow money from his father. It wasn't easy, but he got the business going.

Phil Knight began selling Tiger sneakers out of the trunk of his car at high school and college track meets. Sales exploded, and by 1969, sales had hit $300,000. Even though sales took off, he ran into cash flow issues. In his book *Shoe Dog*, Knight states, "The accountant in me saw risk, the entrepreneur saw the possibility." His bankers felt his rate of growth was too fast. Phil's lack of equity was an issue.

Phil responded by saying, "That is the price of business growth; you don't tell a runner in a race that he's running too fast."

That didn't work, and the bank dropped him as a client. Phil was desperate and finally got financing from Nissho, a Japanese trading company that was doing $100 billion in sales at the time. They loved growth companies with a big upside.

> "An entrepreneur is someone who will jump off a cliff and assemble an airplane on the way down."
>
> — Reid Hoffman

Blue Ribbon Sports couldn't import Tiger shoes after a legal battle, so in 1972, it rebranded itself as Nike and began making and selling their own shoes. Nike was the Greek goddess of victory. Phil and his team realized the new brand needed its own logo. Nike's "swoosh" logo, now considered one of the most recognized logos in the world, was commissioned for $35 from a graphic design student at Portland State University, the same university where Phil taught accounting.

When asked what the swoosh meant, Phil replied, "It's the sound of someone going past you."

Nike shoes came in orange shoe boxes, when white or blue were standard colours. Phil felt orange was the boldest colour in the rainbow and that the shoe boxes would pop on the shelves of the sporting goods stores.

Nike's sales rose 50 percent in 1973 to $4.8 million. Nike shoes were now manufactured in Japan, Taiwan, Korea, and Puerto Rico. The speed at which Nike was growing was incredible.

Since 2005, Nike's gross profit margin has averaged 45 percent. As mentioned earlier, the higher the gross profit margin, the better. This explains how profitable their business model is.

The entrepreneur will ask, "Does it make sense to import running shoes from Asia and sell them in North America?" Phil Knight did his analysis and knew it made financial sense.

Adidas is Nike's main competitor. Adidas had dominated the shoe market for decades before Nike showed up. Adidas is like Eobard Thawne (Reverse-Flash), the archenemy of the Flash. Nike's market cap is $165 billion, almost five times larger than Adidas. Under Armour is worth just under $4 billion. That puts into perspective just how much larger Nike is compared to its competitors. Nike's gross profit margins are higher than its competitors. They have sales, but they keep a close eye on their production costs.

When you begin investing in stocks, it's a good idea to compare financial ratios of competitors and companies in other sectors. Your money can be invested anywhere, so don't limit your investment options to one industry or sector. For example, Ford's gross profit margins average 13 percent, which are much lower than Nike's. Let's see why that is important if you are an investor:

Nike Market Cap: $165 billion (2023)
Ford Market Cap: $56 billion (2023)

2019 Income Statements (Pre-Covid Results)

	Nike	Ford
Revenue:	$39 billion	$156 billion
Gross Profit:	$17.5 billion	$21 billion
Gross Profit Margin:	45%	13.5%

Nike is worth three times more than Ford, even though Ford's revenue (sales) is four times higher than Nike's. You must always look at past sales. It's Nike's high-profit margin that gets investors' attention.

As you go further down the income statement, you need to subtract all the selling, general, and administrative expenses associated with the business. This reveals how the executive team chooses to spend the money. For example, Ford executives might decide to spend billions of dollars a year on making and distributing *Fast and Furious* rip-off movies with Ford cars instead of Dodges, thinking it might increase sales. Similarly, Nike could choose to pay Kanye West a billion dollars a year to wear their shoes, but this can backfire when he opens his mouth. I am looking at you, Adidas! These decisions are made by people in boardrooms. If companies don't watch their expenses, they can become like runaway trains. It could end badly.

This is why the company's EBIT number is important. Earnings Before Interest and Taxes measures the profit a company generates from its operations. It is often used to value a business. You get:

2019 Nike EBIT: $4.8 billion
2019 Ford EBIT: $574 million

It is more profitable to sell Air Jordans than Ford Mustangs and F-150s. The difference is literally in the billions.

This is why many investors avoid companies like Ford. The sales may be high, but the profits are not, which helps explain why Ford's stock in 2023 is worth the same as it was in 1997: $14 a share. Also, a small reduction in sales can wipe out profits.

Nike stock was trading around $10 a share in 2005. It paid a dividend of $0.12 a share. Most investors thought there was no room left to grow. After all, Michael Jordan—basketball superstar and the face of Nike—retired in 2003.

Nike stock price is $107 a share today. The annual dividend is now $1.36 a share. I wonder what the top investment bankers who thought Nike just couldn't grow when it was at $10 a share fifteen years ago are thinking now, when they see how much the stock has grown.

Jordan helped transform Nike from a scrappy underdog into one of the largest, most valuable consumer brands in the world.

The funny thing is, Nike wasn't his first choice. Initially, he wanted to sign with Adidas. The Air Jordan lineup is popular and profitable because of the branding power behind them. They're marketed as luxury goods but targeted to everyone from elementary-age school kids to seniors working out in gyms. The Jordan brand had a revenue of $3.1 billion in the fiscal year ending May 2019. According to *Forbes*, Michael Jordan made $130 million in 2019 off the Air Jordan brand. Jordan's shoe money alone is more than the $127 million in total earnings made by Lionel Messi, who is ranked as the world's highest-paid athlete this year. Michael Jordan makes more money sitting at home than current athletes who are at the top of their game. It's been seventeen years since Jordan shot a basketball in an NBA game.

Celebrity endorsements have been key to Nike's ongoing success. After Jordan, they struck big again by signing athletes such as Tiger Woods, Kobe Bryant, and LeBron James in the early stages of their career.

> "The cowards never started, and the weak died along the way. That leaves us, ladies and gentlemen."
>
> — Phil Knight

Phil Knight used a low-cost strategy to ensure Nike was profitable. This ensured his company could grow sales at a record pace while he still maintained control. What good is speed if you have no control? Ford Mustangs are powerful cars that are rear-wheel drive, but they lose control if the driver loses focus and accelerates too quickly on slick surfaces. What worked for Phil Knight was that he was a runner like the Flash. Runners know that when you focus on the finish line and give it 100 percent, everything around you becomes a blur. It all becomes about speed and control.

FIFTEEN
BCE: Men in suits report to people in pajamas?

"Men in suits look real impressive until you
find out they work for people in pajamas."

— Unknown

Back in 2011, BCE (in partnership with Rogers Communications) purchased the NHL's Toronto Maple Leafs and the NBA's Toronto Raptors for $1.3 billion. The main reason for the purchase was to own the rights to stream live content for their sports channels, digital properties, and smartphones.

The press release stated, "People have wireless devices like smartphones and tablets, and they want to watch live sports. Advertisers pay a premium for such viewers. Nobody wants to watch a game two days later."

Fast forward to June 14, 2019, and George Cope, CEO of BCE, with the Raptors management team, watched game six in Oracle Arena in Oakland, California. The Toronto Raptors beat the Golden State Warriors and won the series. This was the Toronto Raptors' (and Canada's) first NBA championship title.

The Toronto Raptors and the Maple Leafs are worth more than $8 billion today. This confirms that BCE buying the teams in 2011 was a smart business decision.

We bought BCE stock to add to the Young Guns Capital Corp. account. It's Canada's largest and oldest telecom carrier. Here are some facts about BCE as of today (2023):

Market Capitalization (what the company is worth): $55 billion
2022 Revenue (sales): $18.5 billion
2022 Net Earnings: $3 billion
Dividend yield: 6.65%

BCE owns Bell Canada, Virgin Mobile, Virgin Radio stations, BNN Bloomberg, TSN, CTV, Toronto Raptors, and the Toronto Maple Leafs.

In the United States, a similar but much larger telecom company is AT&T, with a market cap of $105 billion. Its 2022 revenue was $121 billion, and it currently has a dividend yield of 7.57 percent. AT&T owns DC Comics, which owns iconic characters such as Superman, Batman, the Flash, and Wonder Woman. It also owns TV shows, including *Green Arrow, The Flash, Supergirl,* and *Black Lightning.*

Superman and Batman have to report to the suits at AT&T, who then have to make the shareholders happy. This explains why superhero movies continue to get produced and released every summer.

We focus and buy shares of companies like BCE because they have a history of growing their dividends over time. BCE paid its first dividend in 1881 and hasn't missed a payment since. In fact, BCE has increased its dividend per share for fourteen consecutive years.

Publicly traded corporations, such as BCE, are made up mainly of shareholders/lenders, managers, and employees.

If you are a shareholder, whether in pajamas or Air Jordan/ Raptors gear—like most teens—all employees and managers, including the CEO, ultimately report to you.

BCE distributes most of its profits (more than 60 percent) in payouts to shareholders. Every day, almost fourty thousand employees and managers at BCE go to work and make this happen. They work hard to increase sales, keep costs down, and make tough business decisions daily.

BCE is able to consistently raise dividends because the corporation runs multiple businesses that generate cash in both good and bad times. For example, almost half of BCE's sales and profit comes from their cell phone division. People love their cell phones and use lots of data, which is great for BCE shareholders.

If they succeed, the dividend grows, and the stock price also increases. So far, they have done a great job. The BCE dividend yield was between 6 to 7 percent when we bought it. Most bank accounts paid less than 1 percent interest at the time, which is why investing in stocks during the pandemic made sense. However, interest rates have increased lately. Our BCE dividends get deposited into our bank account every three months.

BCE isn't the kind of company that will make you rich overnight, but over the long term, it should continue to do well. Anyone can buy shares in companies like BCE and be shareholders in pajamas, while the people in suits report to us.

SIXTEEN
Investing in Railroads: Double-Digit Returns Since 1995

When discussing stocks at parties, everyone likes to talk about hot companies that are in the news, such as Tesla, Netflix, and Amazon. The annoying ones don't stop talking about Bitcoin.

I have yet to have someone come up to me and say, "I like railroad stocks such as Canadian National Railway. They're a boring, safe way to earn double-digit returns year after year." I will discuss this later in the article, but first, you need to know the history of railroads in North America.

The railroad was first developed in the early 1800s in Great Britain by a man named George Stephenson. George never went to school, but at eighteen, he taught himself to read, write, and do basic arithmetic. Gifted with an engineering mind, he successfully applied the steam technology of the day and created the world's first successful locomotive. At the time, George had no idea just how his invention was going to change the world.

> The railroad was a new technology, an industrial version of the Internet requiring continuous innovation. Railroads spurred extraordinary feats

of engineering. Nature had to be re-sculptured; tunnels had to be dug and bridges mounted over precipices. The transcontinental required an 800-foot-long, 63-foot-deep cut through a pass in the Sierra Nevada; it was blasted through at the pace of a foot a day. The tracks also passed along the edges of the rocky walls of a cliff 2,500 feet above a ravine.

—"The Transcontinental Railroad as the Internet of 1869" by Edward Rothstein, *The New York Times*

Figure 10 - An empty eastbound CP Rail unit coal train crosses Stoney Creek Bridge - 8 Sept 1988 John West

Like the Internet, railways forged previously unthinkable connections and opened up new opportunities for commerce. Railroads became popular because they reduced the cost of shipping by carriage by 60 to 70 percent. This makes sense. Imagine trying to ship lumber across the country by horse and carriage. It was expensive and time-consuming. Commodities, such as grain, lumber, oil, and coal, could be shipped in days rather than weeks.

In some cases, hours instead of days. The introduction of railroads explains the rapid expansion of the North American economy.

Shipping and railroad tycoon Cornelius "Commodore" Vanderbilt (1794–1877) dropped out of school at the age of eleven. When Vanderbilt began his career, there were no railroads. He made his fortune in the steamship industry, but in the 1860s, he shifted his focus to the railroads.

Vanderbilt provided the first rail service between New York and Chicago. His company revolutionized rail operations by standardizing procedures and timetables, increasing efficiency, and decreasing travel and shipment times.

In the mid-1800s, the US population was moving west, and train service was the ideal mode of transportation. It was cheaper and quicker than the alternatives available at the time. Vanderbilt took advantage of the situation and made a fortune. When Vanderbilt died, railroads had become the greatest force in modern industry. Vanderbilt was the richest man in Europe and America and the largest owner of railroads in the world. His net worth would have been more than $200 billion in today's dollars.

> "Any fool can make a fortune; It takes a man of brains to hold onto it after it is made."
>
> — Cornelius Vanderbilt

The greatest irony is that the Vanderbilt family were terrible at managing money, and within just fifty years of Cornelius's death, the Vanderbilt family fortune was completely gone. The Vanderbilts are best remembered for displaying their wealth by erecting opulent mansions—ten of them on Manhattan's Fifth Avenue—and throwing extravagant parties on a regular basis that would put the Great Gatsby to shame. They were more interested in spending rather than investing and growing their net worth.

The Great Depression hit in the 1930s, and eventually, most of the money was gone.

Most ultrawealthy families live by the financial advice "Save the principal, spend the interest." Unfortunately, the Vanderbilts never followed that advice and paid a heavy price for it, literally. They should have kept their railroad stocks and lived off the dividends.

In Canada, railroad stocks, such as Canadian National (CN) Railway and Canadian Pacific Kansas City Limited (CP) have been fantastic investments over the past twenty-plus years.

As their website states, "CN Rail stock has increased at a compound annual growth rate of 16% since our initial public offering in 1995." Incredible, yet nobody talks about this. Not even investment professionals. Annual double-digit returns for twenty-eight years is a fantastic investment, yet nobody pays attention.

In 2003, CN's share price was around $11. Today, it's around $157 per shares.

Similarly, the annual dividend was $0.32 per share back in 2003, and it has increased to $3.16 per share now.

Annualized High Double-Digit Capital and Dividend Growth

Most people get annual pay raises in the 2 to 3 percent range, and banks pay less than 1 percent interest for money left in savings accounts.

Canada has a rail duopoly, where two firms have dominant or exclusive control over a market. CN and CP are the only options for companies to ship products via rail. It is impossible for a billionaire or another company to come in and set up a railway. Good luck trying to lay track in just one city, let alone in a country like Canada. It's not just the billions it would require in start-up costs, but also the process of obtaining all the legal, government, and environmental approvals that makes it an impossible task. Nobody wants a rail line in their backyard, especially after a runaway train carrying crude oil derailed and exploded in 2013 in Lac-Mégantic, Quebec, killing forty-seven people. It made national headlines. Look how difficult it is just to build pipelines in North America.

According to Howard Green's book *Railroader* (the best book on the rail industry), the construction of CP Railroad (now the CPKC) had been financed and backed by the federal government. CP received twenty-five million acres of government land. Hundreds of Chinese workers died constructing the railway in Canada, and Indigenous communities ceded control of their land. I don't think anyone adhered to any strict environmental regulations when they were blowing up mountains in Western Canada to lay rail tracks.

> "They ain't buildin' any more railroads. Critical infrastructure was constructed decades, if not more than a century ago, as cities built up around rail lines. The only way for existing railroads to get bigger and more efficient was to swallow others."
>
> – Hunter Harrison, author of *Railroader*

Hunter was a famous and respected CEO who turned around four struggling North American railroads, including CN and CP.

This is important. Bill Gates's (Microsoft) and Warren Buffett's (Berkshire Hathaway) combined net worth is over $200 billion. They are two of the wealthiest people on the planet. These two working together would not be able to build a new railway for all the reasons listed above, and they know this. That is why Berkshire Hathaway paid $26 billion for Burlington Northern Santa Fe (BNSF) back in 2009.

BNSF operates one of the largest freight railroad networks in North America, with more than 52,000 km of rail across the United States. At one time, Bill Gates and his family owned more than 15 percent of all CN shares, making them the largest shareholder. It is difficult to say how much Bill owns now, after his divorce settlement. There is a reason these two men are consistently ranked among the top five richest people in the world.

CN has been our favourite. It's been a fantastic rail operator that has been deemed North America's most efficient railway. It was owned by the Government of Canada until 1995, when it became a public company, and anyone could buy shares. CN's market capitalization was just over $2 billion then. It is now $106 billion.

Their moat—a distinct advantage a company has over its competitors, which allows it to protect its market share and profitability—literally spans 30,000 km of tracks across Canada and Central America, starting from the Atlantic and Pacific oceans to the Gulf of Mexico. CN is one of the few railroads on the continent with access to all three coastlines, ranging from the US Midwest to the Gulf Coast region, giving it a competitive advantage over its peers. Hundreds of billions of dollars in goods move between the United States and Canada. Check out their rail map.

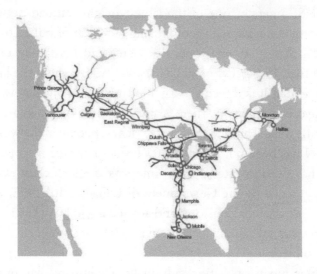

Figure 11 - Map of CN Rail Network (www.cn.ca), April. 15, 2022

Canada's rail network is an essential part of the economy. Rail stocks tend to do well when the economy is expanding and growing. Warren Buffet explained his purchase of Burlington Northern during the 2009 recession: "I just basically believe this country will prosper, and you'll have more people moving more goods ten and twenty and thirty years from now, and the rails should benefit." So far, he has been right. Consumption continues to increase as people keep buying more stuff.

CN transports over $250 billion worth of freight every year, comprising automotive components, chemicals, crude oil, wheat, and more. As well, 95 percent of grain exports in Canada are transported by rail. One car of grain can be worth as much as $30,000. Next time you see a train go by, count the rail cars. If CN is transporting commodities, such as oil, lumber, or other goods, the value of each car increases. A railroad is often viewed as a recession-proof business.

Hunter Harrison said, "Railroads only make money when cars are moving. Track is a railroad's most expensive physical asset."

Railroads have been getting significantly better at controlling their expenses by reducing their tracks, creating leaner labour forces, and building longer and heavier trains. All this leads to better operating ratios and more profits. The railroad's main competitor is the trucking industry.

In 2019, CN had revenues of $14.9 billion and a net income of $4.2 billion. Its operating ratio (OR), the key measure of railroad performance, was 62.5 percent. Every time a railroad releases its quarterly numbers, investors want to know if the OR is increasing or decreasing. It shows how efficient a company's management is at keeping costs low while generating sales. The smaller the ratio, the more efficient the company.

In railroading, an OR of eighty or lower is considered desirable. If it's in the high nineties, it means the railroad has spent everything it has generated in sales. It is not a good place for any business to be.

For every $1 in sales, CN generates $0.375 in profit (before interest, taxes, depreciation, and amortization).

Have you ever played Monopoly? In the game of Monopoly, the rent for railroads depends on how many railroads the player owns. If you own one, the rent on it is $25. If you own two, you can collect $50 in rent from anyone landing on either. If you own three, then you get $100, and if you own all four railroads, the rent is $200. Nobody ever got rich owning railroad stocks in Monopoly; you can't build houses or hotels on them. However, most people don't realize that railroads are highly lucrative investments in real life.

SEVENTEEN
Invest in Airlines?
Seriously?

We've explained the rationale about the companies we have invested in, but there is one sector we would not invest in: airlines. Sometime in the early 1980s, Richard Branson, British entrepreneur, and owner of Virgin Records, was on his way to the British Virgin Islands to meet his girlfriend when his American Airlines flight was suddenly cancelled.

Nothing was going to stop Richard that day, so he marched to the back of the airport, gave them his credit card, and hired a plane. He then borrowed a blackboard, wrote "Virgin Airlines one-way: $39 to the Virgin Islands," and filled up the flight with all the bumped passengers. The next day, he called Boeing and said, "I've just had a bad experience, and I'm thinking of starting an airline called Virgin. Do you have any second-hand 747s for sale?"

Fast forward to 2019, Virgin Atlantic Airways' revenue was almost three billion British pounds. Its thirty-seven aircrafts flew roughly 5.6 million passengers around the world that year. What a business success story.

Airlines sound like a great investment, so then why is Richard Branson famously quoted as saying: "If you want to be a millionaire, start with a billion dollars and launch a new airline"?

Air travel remains a low-margin business because most travellers prioritize price above all else. Booking cheap flights online doesn't help the airlines. It is also capital-intensive. Modern aircraft, jet fuel, and experienced crew aren't cheap. Airlines are ultrasensitive to things they have no control over, such as oil prices or a global pandemic that shuts down air traffic. I am looking at you, COVID-19!

In 2019, US airlines posted their tenth straight year of profits and were preparing for even more growth in travel demand in 2020. Then COVID-19 started to spread. US travel demand dropped by 95 percent in 2020. Ouch.

The future of air travel looked bleak. In 2020, Richard Branson had offered his Caribbean luxury island resort as collateral to secure a UK government bailout for his struggling airline, Virgin Atlantic Airways. I guess his quote makes a lot of sense now.

Warren Buffett, billionaire value investor, sold his entire position in the US airline industry. His prior stake, which was worth north of $4 billion in December 2019, included positions in United, American, Southwest, and Delta Air Lines. In most cases, Buffett owned 10 percent of all outstanding stock in these airlines. That is a huge stake, and it made headlines when he sold all his stock in airlines.

Today many businesses across the globe have adapted to Zoom meetings and other modes of communication instead of travelling.

Business travel is a profitable segment for airlines. If an executive needs to be in Toronto or New York next week for an important meeting, they are not necessarily concerned about getting the cheapest flight, especially if the company is paying for it.

However, with the shift to virtual meetings, the previous level of business travel may not return. This is a potential risk.

Airline stocks don't do well over the long-term, except for WestJet and Southwest Airlines; they are meant to be traded like commodity stocks. Buy them when they are low and out of favour then sell them when the economy is doing great. We decided not to invest in them.

EIGHTEEN
Dividend Income

"Following's not really my style."

— Tony Stark

People who have seen the *Ironman* movies know Tony Stark is a genius inventor, billionaire, former playboy, and majority owner of Stark Industries. CNN Money estimated Tony Stark's wealth at $12.4 billion; he's one of the richest superheroes.

Stark Industries is primarily a defence company that develops and manufactures advanced weapons and military technologies. It is a publicly traded company listed on the New York Stock Exchange, so anyone can buy shares. According to the comic books, the company does pay a regular dividend.

Tony makes money off dividends and when the stock price goes up (capital appreciation). Tony wakes up every day and does whatever he wants, inventing new gadgets, weapons, modifying his Ironman suit, then racing in his Audi to his private jet to a cool party somewhere in the world.

You don't see him waking up at 6:00 a.m., cooking breakfast, making his lunch, getting stuck in traffic driving to work, then sitting in a cubicle or a boring office meeting while dealing with an angry boss.

Dividends from large, well-known companies (let's say Stark Industries) tend to be more stable than their stock prices. This is because even during down markets, many companies will continue to pay and even grow their dividends. The key is to diversify and own many companies in different industries. That is why we own BCE, Royal Bank, Suncor Energy, Starbucks, Disney, Nike, Google, and CN Rail. These stocks have a strong history of raising dividends or reinvesting in their businesses.

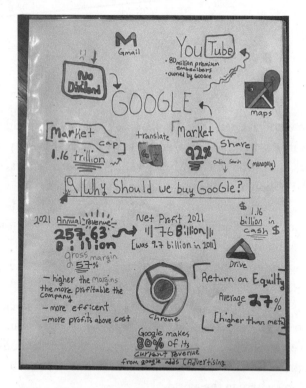

Figure 12 – We did our own analysis of Google. They own 92 percent in online search. We like to do one page write ups on companies we want to invest in. If we can't fit it on one page and explain it like this example, then we are not going to invest.

Dividend income is more tax-efficient than salary income. This is important because taxes suck up a lot of your money. The average Canadian makes just over $50,000 a year ($26 per hour) working full time.

If you made $50,000 a year working full time at a job, then you would pay at least $11,000 a year in income taxes. There are also work-related expenses, such as a car (car payments, insurance, and gas) and professional clothes that are not cheap. This could be another $10,000 in work-related expenses a year. You now have $29,000 left over to cover all your expenses, which is not much.

Someone who earns $50,000 in dividends (from Canadian stocks) in Canada essentially pays no income tax. Additionally, if they don't have to go to work, they do not have work-related costs. This person would have $50,000 to cover all their expenses. The government encourages you to earn dividend income. Just ask an accountant to confirm.

We can't all be Tony Stark, but we can all invest in publicly traded companies and collect dividends. The capital appreciation is a nice add-on.

Money is a superpower because it gives you the freedom to do what you want. You wake up every day and focus on what makes you happy. You can work at a job you like, which may pay less than a job you hate, but you need it to pay your monthly bills.

NINETEEN
Investing and Building a Superhero Body

A very strange thing happened during the COVID-19 pandemic. People began investing in cryptocurrencies, meme stocks, NFTs and land sales in the metaverse. Most people could not explain these investments, but everyone was talking about them. Who is Satoshi Nakamoto? Did he really create Bitcoin in 2008? Why has no one ever seen him/her/them? The questions are endless. Anyways global travel came to a halt during the pandemic, and no one needed to rent cars at airports. Car rental company Hertz Global Holdings filed for bankruptcy but shares of the company shot up. The investment community was stunned and couldn't explain it. Usually, when companies declare bankruptcy, their shares go to zero and wipe out shareholders. The company itself warned that "the shares are worthless."

So, what happened here?

People who were recently laid off or were working from home started investing and buying shares of Hertz. This dramatically increased the share price. Over a span of three weeks, the stock shot up from 56 cents to $5.53 a share—a tenfold return. Some sold high and took profits. They then posted to social media sites and YouTube, explaining how easy it is to make money in the stock market. As a general rule, never take investment advice from a weird dude on YouTube. This is the same crowd who were regulars at casinos and did a fair amount of sports betting before COVID-19. With everything closed, these people found a new outlet.

> "The stock market has a way of schooling people who think they have this investing thing all figured out. Stock market rallies and investing fads all end, and they often end ugly."
>
> — Rob Carrick, *The Globe and Mail Reporter*

Hertz stock dropped from $5.53 to $1.47 per share. Once one of the largest car rental companies, Hertz filed for Chapter 11 bankruptcy protection on May 22, 2020. The company had more than $18 billion in debt. I would hate to be the person who bought the stock at $5 dollars and thought it would go higher.

This story is all too familiar. These people take a large sum of money and invest it in companies they have never heard of. Or even if they have, they don't review the company's financial statements themselves. Someone (usually on YouTube, Instagram, a family member, or a friend) tells them there is no risk and they will make a fortune in weeks, if not days. They buy, then the stock drops shortly after and they sell in a panic, taking a huge loss. These people then swear to never invest in stocks again.

Investing in stocks for the short term is like gambling. Anything can happen. Any stock can suddenly go up or down for any or no reason at all. You are no better off than gambling in a casino.

Investing, in my opinion, is very similar to building a superhero body.

You are not going to start your first gym session attempting to bench-press 300 pounds because you saw Hugh Jackman do it in an Instagram post. The weight will land hard on your chest and seriously injure you.

Actors who played superheroes, such as Superman, Thor, Wolverine, Aquaman, and Captain America, have trained hard and focused on their diets for years. They have also had access to the best trainers money can buy.

There is no "Super Soldier Serum" that can turn Steve Rogers from a weak and frail little thing, deemed unfit for military service, into Captain America in minutes.

Chris Evans has played Captain America in several movies. He was in great shape to begin with, but to look like a superhero, he had to significantly increase his protein intake and stop all cardio. He hit the gym six days a week for three months, training for two hours a day. The training program was based on heavy-weight/low-rep sets of the classic compound lifts: squats, deadlifts, shoulder press, bench press, weighted dips, and chin-ups. These are incredibly tough exercises to do, and it takes time to see results.

All of this is not rocket science in terms of workout and diet tips. In fact, it is very basic weightlifting 101 stuff. The challenge is to push yourself through the pain and be consistent. Work out on days you don't want to. Eat fish and vegetables when people around you are eating pizza. This is where most people either fail or succeed in their diets and workout plans.

Occasionally, you might come up with new information that might change your mind about your workout routine. Have you ever heard of Sergio Oliva? Sergio was a weightlifter and a member of the Cuban delegation that went to the 1962 Pan American Games in Jamaica. He used the opportunity to break away from the team and fled to Chicago (at that time, Cuba's citizens practically never received exit permits). He came to the United States and then started bodybuilding. He won the Mr.

Olympia title from 1967 to 1969: three consecutive times! He was a powerhouse, bench-pressing 525 pounds.

Arnold Schwarzenegger and the rest of the competitors couldn't figure out how he had such perfect abs and V shape, even though they all did the same exercises. What was his secret? Later, they discovered he was a terrific baseball player, and that's what helped his waist: tens of thousands of reps twisting to swing a bat.

Mike Mentzer was the first man ever to achieve a perfect score in the 1978 Mr. Universe competition. In the 1950s and 1960s, fitness magazines often featured high-volume, high-frequency training programs that neglected to consider the genetic advantages of elite bodybuilders. Every title winner was training six days a week for at least two hours a day, including Arnold Schwarzenegger.

Mentzer believed many bodybuilders were "overtraining," so he emphasized brief, high-intensity, and infrequent workouts. Mentzer's workouts were often forty-five minutes in duration, and he only trained three days a week. As we mentioned earlier in the book, investing, like weightlifting, is a personal journey. Everyone is different, and you need to be aware of that.

Investing in stocks is the equivalent to weightlifting. You need to be patient and work at it. Your muscles will be sore at first, and you may not see much progress in the beginning. Keep at it and think long term. You will learn a lot in the process.

If you want to be successful in investing, you must be patient and have a long-term view. Think in terms of five to ten years, not a few weeks. Some goals take time to achieve, such as building a superhero body.

Anyone can become a shareholder. The key is to start early, invest in large companies you know, diversify your portfolio, and think long term.

"Successful investing takes time, discipline, and patience. No matter how great the talent or effort, some things just take time: You can't produce a baby in one month by getting nine women pregnant."

— Warren Buffett, billionaire investor who bought his first stock at age eleven

TWENTY
Young Guns Is a Success and Gives Back to the Community.

"Half of what separates successful entrepreneurs from
unsuccessful ones is pure perseverance."

— Steve Jobs

Consistency is harder to maintain when no one is clapping for
you. You must keep going despite the setbacks. Athletes who
reach the elite level understand and live by the saying, "Rent
is due every day!" With Young Guns WC, we wanted to make
fitness accessible for all youth and provide a fun group environment focused on proper technique. A strong body is not made
in comfort. You must push yourself beyond your comfort zone
because that's where the gains lie, whether it's in the gym or in
life. We tell the youth in our program that it doesn't get easier,
they just become stronger.

We had many setbacks and learned a lot along the way. At one
point, due to COVID-19 restrictions, we were not even allowed
to sell our high-protein donuts or merchandise directly to the

public. We couldn't accept cash. Until that point, Young Guns WC had managed to sustain itself by selling club merchandise, offering high-protein donuts, and securing community grants for funding. With no budget, our Instagram page became our key marketing tool. Social media can be a powerful tool for good if used effectively.

COVID-19 and its variants shut down large public gatherings, including fundraising galas. Many nonprofits fund their operations from the money raised at their galas. With restrictions on large gatherings easing in 2022, we held our Bollywood Boom Fundraising Gala in April. The event was almost cancelled due to a surge in COVID-19 infections, but luckily, public events were allowed to proceed. Over 350 people attended the event, and some people even flew in from out-of-province. It was one of the largest fundraising galas in the area at the time. Many people hadn't attended a party in years. We raised $39,700.

All the event's proceeds went straight to the club. We were humbled by the support we received, and it was great to see the donors dance the night away. The funds helped us buy more shares of the companies listed above. We were closer to making the club sustainable without the need for grants or fundraising. This has always been our goal.

Our club and our success did not go unnoticed in the community. Young Guns were featured in the business section of *The Globe and Mail*, a national publication, and we were awarded the 2021 Fraser Valley Cultural Diversity Award for Innovative Initiative (small organizations). The Diversity Awards is one of the largest galas in the Fraser Valley, with key individuals from various communities in attendance. It was moved online the year we won due to the COVID-19 pandemic. Recently, we were awarded a Community Service Award (Under Age 25) by the City of Mission. We were told this is the highest honour the city can give its citizens. Receiving our award in a packed theatre, with everyone clapping and cheering, was an indescribable feeling.

Our biggest accomplishment to date was advocating for a new high school in our community. The current high school was more than seventy years old, overcapacity, and unsafe. The province had rejected the school board's initial proposal for a new high school. The community was extremely upset. They had been trying to secure a new high school for twenty years. In addition, our local provincial representatives had promised us a new high school if we voted for them. We did vote for them, and they were elected, but no new high school was delivered.

Being self-funded gave us the freedom to do whatever we wanted without any funding constraints. For example, we were able to publicly advocate for a new high school, while many non-profits and community groups chose not to do so as they rely on grants and funding from the same branch of government we were fighting against. We were respectful and fact-based. There were no personal attacks. We needed to use our voice and brand power in the community to get the government to change their mind. We referenced the government's own new school construction and shared press releases on social media confirming that new schools were being built and approved in other communities, but not in ours.

We did our research and engaged the community to demand our fair share from local politicians and the Ministry of Education. We made marketing material and distributed it in the community during large-scale public events and regularly on social media. We had meetings with members of the opposition party. We needed them to push the government to keep their last election promise. We even held a rally and brought in a 1952 GMC truck—it was towed—to show people the school was the same age as the truck and to show all the technological and life-saving improvements that have been made to cars since. Seat belts in that model were optional. We made custom T-shirts for the event, which became popular on social media. We even sent a few to the minister and deputy minister of education. We talked to local candidates in the municipal election and made the new high school a key issue. Many of them attended our rally. We did our very best and campaigned hard for nine months.

Recently, the provincial government announced that we would get a new $130-million high school. It's hard to describe in words how it felt. The next generation of kids will learn in a new modern high school that is not only environmentally friendly, but also a place to prepare students for twenty-first-century careers.

Figure 13 – Our hard work paid off. Mission will get a new $130-million high school. Many in the community helped make this happen; some have been working on this project for twenty years. We did our part.

Because of our investment returns, we were able to donate to many community projects and organizations. In several years, we went from asking for donations to making donations. Our donation process was streamlined to talking to a few people involved in the cause and then simply sending them an e-transfer. Many people in the community had done this with us, so we wanted to return the favour. Here are some of the organizations and projects that we were able to contribute to:

- helped the community food bank raise $1,000 through donut fundraisers.
- funded a local university food bank.
- donated to several schools' breakfast/snack programs.
- sponsored new jerseys for the local middle school boys' basketball team. The boys went on to have one of the best seasons in their school's history.
- donated to various youth sports teams' fundraisers and tournaments.
- donated to the purchase of a CT scanner for a local hospital.
- donated to the Hospice Gala fundraisers.
- donated to our local search and rescue team.
- purchased a blood pressure machine and three pocket talkers for the local seniors' clinic.

The youth in our weightlifting program have dominated at the provincial and national levels. One of our youths, a seventeen-year-old, broke twelve powerlifting records in two age classes at national and provincial levels at the 2022 Canadian Powerlifting League competition in Nanton, Alberta. In powerlifting, a lifter has nine attempts to achieve the highest total possible. A lifter gets three attempts each for squat, bench press, and deadlift. The goal is to lift the maximum amount of weight for one repetition. Gaurav Dhanoa achieved an impressive 1,038 pounds across all three lifts: a squat of 336 pounds, a bench press of 228 pounds, and a deadlift of 474 pounds. Gaurav's picture made it into the local paper. We were all so proud. It's amazing to see what proper support can do for today's youth.

Louis "The Mission Kid" Latour brought home a silver medal at the 2023 Canadian Powerlifting Union National Championships. Latour finished in second place with a 628-pound squat, a 413-pound bench press, and a 700-pound deadlift. Last year, Louis finished just outside the podium and placed fourth nationally. The 2022 event was held in St. John's, Newfoundland.

The interesting thing is we met Louis when we first began selling our club T-shirts door to door. We mentioned to him that he should participate in powerlifting competitions, and we would support him. He did, and we also kept our promise.

Just recently, Louis was selected to represent Canada at the 2023 North American Powerlifting Championships, which took place in the Cayman Islands in August 2023. To fund the trip, and his training, we began selling our protein donuts again. This time, Louis finished first. He set the Canadian national record with 464-pound bench press and a 727-pound deadlift. We were so proud.

Mohit Parmar placed second at the 2023 Nationals and benched 352 pounds. He made huge gains from the 2022 Nationals when he benched 314 pounds and came in sixth.

Young Guns' recent powerlifting champion is eighteen-year-old Manohar Panesar. He broke four provincial (British Columbia) powerlifting records and won the best overall lifter award. He weighed only 142 pounds, but went on to squat 409 pounds, bench-press 270 pounds, and deadlift 507 pounds. All of his lifts were done with perfect form.

Young Guns helped cover part of these athletes' training, travel, and competition costs. We hope these stories can provide inspiration to anyone hoping to chase their dreams and compete at a high level.

Figure 14 - We received the 2022 Community Service award in the Under 25 category from the City of Mission. We were told it was the highest honour your city can give you.

Keeping youth engaged and active is an ongoing issue in our communities. In creating an environment where it is safe—from both an emotional and a physical injury perspective—to lift weights and throw a punch, Young Guns goal is to teach young people how to be strong, confident, disciplined, and proud of who they are. By turning Young Guns WC into a social enterprise and investing our funds in blue-chip, dividend-paying stocks, we were able to pay for our club costs without relying on grants or fundraising. We achieved freedom. With that freedom, we were able to take the club to new heights and deliver results.

In our final note, and last reference to superheroes, we would like to discuss the Batmobile, which has always been a cool part of the Batman movies. Batman does not have superhuman powers like Superman and the Flash, so he needed a car to get around Gotham City to fight crime. He needed a very special car.

I like the version in *Batman Begins*. The Batmobile was originally built as an off-road military assault vehicle by Wayne Enterprises. Bruce Wayne got a hold of it and made some major modifications to ensure it could go to war with criminals in Gotham City and evade the police when needed (stealth mode). The car played a key role in saving Rachel Dawes' life when she was poisoned, and it saved Gotham City from certain doom.

The Batmobile had the armour of a tank to protect Batman but could beat a Corvette in a race. Once the Batmobile speed hit 100 mph, it became an unstoppable battering ram. Despite its size, it had to be able to turn corners on a dime. It's not easy driving on downtown streets at high speed. Don't even get me started on the high-powered machine guns and countless missiles. During the movie, its jet engine allowed it to fly when all the bridges into the city were closed. Everyone, including the police, stood by their cars, mesmerized by the sheer awesomeness of the Batmobile, wishing they had one.

Batman's ride was an engineering, automotive, military, and technological marvel. It was a great car for a superhero to employ offensive and defensive strategies when needed. For Young Guns, our blue-chip dividend stocks are our Batmobile. If we would have left the money in a savings account in the bank, then we would have had to fight crime with just Nike running shoes.

An important key to investing, according to Peter Lynch, is to remember that stocks are not lottery tickets. There's a company behind every stock and a reason the stock performs the way it does. Do your research, diversify, and be patient.

Young Guns Weightlifting and Boxing Club offers free coed weightlifting and boxing programs to youth. Pavi Toor and his two teenage sons started the program in September 2019 because they realized that the greatest limitations youth faced when it came to weightlifting was safety, inexperience, and financial resources.

Figure 15 – Young Guns Powerlifting Coach Ryan Maclellan (Center) placed first in the bench press category, lifting 407 pounds at the 2023 National Powerlifting Championships. Mohit Parmar (Right) placed second in the bench press category, lifting 352 pounds in his weight division.

Figure 16 - Powerlifter Gaurav Dhanoa, left, with coach Ryan Maclellan at the Canadian Powerlifting League nationals in Alberta on Aug. 21, 2022. The 17-year-old broke 12 powerlifting records in two age classes, at national and provincial levels.

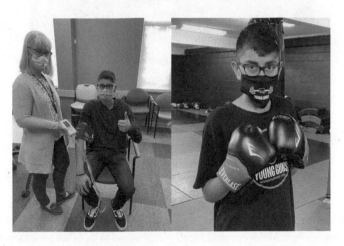

Figure 17 – Young Guns' mask sales were strong during the pandemic. Our club merchandise sales always exceeded our expectations.

Figure 18 – Louis Latour (Center) poses with the Young Guns leadership team. He placed second, overall, in his weight class at the 2023 Canadian Powerlifting Championships in Richmond, British Columbia. He deadlifted an incredible 700 lb. Louis was also mentioned in the local paper.

Figure 19 – Louis Latour helps Sahaj Singh (Below) bench-press. Sahaj was one of the first members of the club when it started back in 2019.

Figure 20 - One of our Young Guns athletes does some off-season training before basketball season starts. We have always encouraged youth athletes to do off-season training. We recommend weightlifting and boxing. Playing the same sport year-round can lead to serious injuries.

Figure 21 - We were honoured to receive the 2021 Innovative Initiative Award (small organizations) at the 18th Annual Fraser Valley Cultural Diversity Awards. Because of COVID restrictions on events and large gatherings at the time, it was a virtual event. Our club gained popularity and credibility in the community after the win.

Figure 22 - Coach Ryan Maclellan stands with Young Guns' newest athlete, Manohar Panesar (Left). Manohar broke four provincial records and received the "Best Lifter" award at the 2023 BC Provincial Powerlifting Championships.

Figure 23 - We shared this poster on social media, distributed it at the New Mission High School Rally we helped organize, and handed it out during community events during the summer. This really got people talking.

Figure 24 – We created and gave these shirts away to everyone to increase awareness about needing a new high school. We even shipped a few to the Ministry of Education leadership team.

Young Guns Is a Success and Gives Back to the Community.

Figure 25 - Young Guns weightlifting program is run by Coach Bailey Dhaliwal. Bailey is a certified trainer and played for the Vancouver Giants hockey team.

Figure 26 - Kultar "Black Mamba" Gill runs the Young Guns boxing/kickboxing program. He is a world renowned and accomplished MMA fighter. He has fought internationally and coached many world champions including in K1, an elite MMA and Kickboxing organization in the world.
Photo: Visual Journalist @jwintsphoto

Bibliography

Books

Buffett, Mary and David Clark. Buffettology: The Previously Unexplained Techniques That Have Made Warren Buffett the World's Most Famous Investor. New York: Rawson Associates, 1997.

Drucker, Peter F. The Drucker Lectures: Essential Lessons On Management, Society, and Economy. New York: McGraw-Hill Books, 2010.

Foster, Derek. The Idiot Millionaire, You Can Become Wealthy. Ottawa: Foster, Underhill Financial Press, 2011.

Green, Howard. Railroader. Toronto: Page Two Books, 2018.

Housel, Morgan. The Psychology Of Money: Timeless Lessons On Wealth, Greed, And Happiness. New York: Harriman House, 2020.

Knight, Phil. Shoe Dog: A memoir by the creator of Nike. New York: Simon & Schuster Books For Young Readers, 2017.

Lynch, Peter. Beating The Street. New York: Simon & Schuster, 1993.

Lynch, Peter. One Up On Wall Street (2nd Edition) . New York: Simon & Schuster, 2000.

Perkins, John. Confessions of an Economic Hit Man. New York: Penguin Group, 2004.

Robbins, Tony. Money Master The Game: 7 Simple Steps To Financial Freedom. New York: Simon & Schuster, 2014.

Schwarzenegger, Arnold. Total Recall: My Unbelievably True Life Story. New York: Simon & Schuster, 2013.

Stanley, Thomas J. and William D. Danko. The Millionaire Next Door: The Surprising Secrets of America's Wealthy. Atlanta: Longstreet Press, Inc. , 1996.

Turner, Garth. Greater Fool: The Troubled Future Of Real Estate. Toronto : Key Porter Books, 2008.

Kiyoski, Robert T. Rich Dad Poor Dad. Scottsdale: Plata Publishing, April 11, 2017.

Movies/TV Shows

Iron Man. Directed by Jon Favreau, Performances by Robert Downey Jr, Marvel Studios, 2008

Captain Marvel. Directed by Anna Boden and Ryan Fleck, Performances by Brie Larson, Marvel Studios, 2019

Smallville. Directed by Alfred Gough and Miles Millar, Performances by Tom Welling, Millar/Gough Ink, Tollin/Robbins Productions, DC Comics and Warner Bros. Television, 2001, based on the DC Comics character Superman created by Jerry Siegel and Joe Schuster.

Marvel's Luke Cage. Created by Cheo Hodari Coker, Performances by Mike Colter, Marvel Television and ABC Studios, 2016, Netflix App

Doctor Strange. Directed by Scott Derrickson, Performances by Benedict Cumberbatch, Marvel Studios/Walt Disney Studios and Motion Pictures, 2016

Black Panther. Directed by Ryan Coogler, Performances by Chadwick Boseman, Marvel Studios, 2018

Avengers. Directed by Joss Whedon, Performances by Robert Downey Jr. and Chris Evans, Marvel Studios, 2012

X-Men. Directed by Bryan Singer, Performances by Hugh Jackman and Patrick Stewart, Marvel Enterprises/20th Century Fox, 2000

Superman. Directed by Richard Donner, Performances by Christopher Reeve, Warner Bros. Pictures, based on the DC Comics character Superman created by Jerry Siegel and Joe Schuster. 1978

Superman Returns. Directed by Bryan Singer, Performances by Brandon Routh, Legendary Pictures/DC Entertainment/Warner Bros. Pictures, 2006

Batman Begins. Directed by Christopher Nolan, Performances by Christian Bale and Michael Caine, Warner Bros. Pictures/DC Comics/Legendary Pictures, 2005

The Flash. Developed by Greg Berlanti, Andrew Kreisberg and Geoff Johns, Performances by Grant Gustin, Bonanza Productions/DC Entertainment/Warner Bros. Television, 2014

Charlie and the Chocolate Factory. Directed by Tim Burton, Performances by Johnny Depp, The Zanuck Company/ Plan B Entertainment/Village Roadshow Pictures, 2005

Teenage Mutant Ninja Turtles. Directed by Steve Barron, Performances by Judith Hoag, Golden Harvest/ Limelight Productions/888 Productions, 1990

Teenage Mutant Ninja Turtles. Created by Kevin Eastman and Peter Laird, Mirage Studios (1984-2009), 1984

The Founder. Directed by John Lee Hancock, Performances by Michael Keaton, Weinstein Company, 2016

Captain America: The First Avenger. Directed by Joe Johnston, Performances by Chris Evans, Marvel Studios, 2011

Articles

Taylor, Bill. "How Domino's Pizza Reinvented Itself." *Harvard Business Review*. November 28, 2016.

_____. "A breakdown of RBC's record $12.9B profit this year, down to the second." *BNN Bloomberg*, December 4, 2019

Schmidt, Ann. "How Fred Smith rescued FedEx from bankruptcy by playing blackjack in Las Vegas." *FOXBusiness*. July 19, 2020.

_____. "The automobile is just a bad investment; it's just a fad." *Portsmouth Herald*. December 19, 2010.

_____. "Harvard, world's wealthiest university, sees endowment soar to $53.2 bln." *Reuters*, October 14, 2021.

Balbi, Danielle. "Harvard's Long Run as Richest College Is Officially Under Threat." *Bloomberg*. August 23, 2022.

Lorin, Janet. "Dartmouth Posts 47% Endowment Return; Fund Rises to $8.5 Billion." *Bloomberg News*. October 11, 2021.

Lorin, Janet. "Penn Endowment Posts 41% Return, Buoyed by Stock Market Gains." *Bloomberg News*. September 23, 2021.

_____. "2006 Annual Report To The Community: Building A Solid Foundation." *Mission Community Foundation*. March 2007.

Turner, Garth. "Trust." *www.greaterfool.ca/blog/*. April 19, 2015.

Peterson, Gunnar. "Buy Stocks Like You Buy Groceries." *The Motley Fool*. May 30, 2014.

Ballard, John. "Here's How Much Warren Buffett Has Made on Coca-Cola." *The Motley Fool*. November 19, 2019.

Healy, Will. "Here's How Much Warren Buffett Has Earned From Coca-Cola's Dividend." *The Motley Fool*. January 27, 2023.

Weaver, Rosanna. "Coca-Cola Needs to Make a Real Change: Shareholders aren't Satisfied with 'We Won't do it Again' pledges." *As You Sow*. April 17, 2023.

Clifford, Catherine. "Coke CEO: Why we have an award for projects that fail." *CNBC*. December 2, 2019.

Potts, Mark. "Coca-Cola Back To Basics With Columbia Sale." *The Washington Post*. September 27, 1989.

_____. "Water becomes America's favorite drink again." *USA Today*. March 11, 2013.

Assis, Claudia. "Pepsi raises dividend by 10%." *MarketWatch*. May 2, 2023.

Elkins, Kathleen. "A janitor secretly amassed an $8 million fortune and left most of it to his library and hospital." *CNBC*. August 29, 2016.

Liew, Christopher. "BMO (TSX:BMO) Has an Insane Dividend Streak of 190 Years." *The Motley Fool*. October 21, 2019.

Carpenter, Scott. "Bill Gates Sells $940 Million of CN Rail Stock, Trimming Stake to 9%." *Bloomberg*. May 13, 2022.

Shapiro, Ariel. "America's Biggest Owner Of Farmland Is Now Bill Gates." *Forbes*. January 14, 2021.

Ignatius, Adi. "The HBR Interview: 'We Had to Own the Mistakes." *Harvard Business Review*. July-August 2010.

Martins, Daniel. "Apple Should Double Its Dividend." *TheStreet*. August 9, 2020.

Faithfull, Mark. "Blockbuster Sends Retro-Fans Into A Frenzy With Cryptic Website Note." *Forbes*. March 27, 2023.

Naysmith, Caleb. "Blockbuster Had The Opportunity To Buy Netflix For $50 Million But 'Laughed Them Out Of The Room' – A $150 Billion Mistake." *Yahoo! Finance*. May 25, 2023.

Burr, Barry B. "GE Nearing $100 Billion Milestone" *Pensions&Investments*. June 26, 1995.

Colvin, Geoff. "For a time, Jack Welch was the most valuable CEO on earth." *Fortune*. March 2, 2020.

Collins, Jim. "Three Bold Actions GE's Board Should Take To Reverse The Stock's Incredible Decline." *Forbes*. September 25, 2018.

Halloran, Richard. "The Sad, Dark End of the British Empire." *Politico Magazine*. August 26, 2014.

Field, Hayden. "Apple's market cap closes above $3 trillion for the first time ever." *CNBC*. June 30, 2023.

Strohmeyer, Robert. "The 7 Worst Tech Predictions of All Time." *PCWorld*. December 31, 2008.

Williams, Sean. "Warren Buffett's $19 Billion Mistake Can Be Your Historic Opportunity." *The Motley Fool*. November 4, 2022.

Barrett, Claire. "The Great North Korean Volvo Heist." *HistoryNet*. February 9, 2023.

Bowenbank, Starr. "Captain Marvel Is the First Female Superhero Movie to Gross $1 Billion Worldwide." *Elle Magazine*. April 4, 2019.

Frankel, Matthew. "S&P 500 Index Defined & Discussed." *The Motley Fool*. April 19, 2023.

Shell, Adam. "How A Creative Physicist Dreamed Up And Created The ETF." *Investor's Business Daily*. February 17, 2022.

Strauss, Lawrence C. "How Bond ETF's Plumbing Can Trip Up Investors When Markets Go Crazy." *Barron's*. March 8, 2023.

_____. "In The Last 30 Years, the SPDR S&P 500 (SPY) ETF obtained a 9.93% compound annual return, with a 14.99% standard deviation." *Lazy Portfolio ETF*. June 30, 2023.

_____. "On its 30th birthday, the ETF looms large." *Vanguard*. February 27, 2023.

Shriber, Todd. "7 ETFs That Aren't for Everybody: There are lots of ETFs in the world, but not all ETFs are intended for every investor." *InvestorPlace*. August 16, 2018.

Foelber, Daniel. "Exxon Removed From the Dow After Nearly 100 Years: What It Means for Investors." *The Motley Fool*. August 31, 2020.

Imbert, Fred. "Stocks post best annual gain in 6 years with the S&P 500 surging more than 28%." *CNBC*. December 31, 2019.

Krauskopf, Lewis. "Tech Titans dominate U.S. stock market after surge." *Reuters*. April 21, 2020.

Daniel, Will. "4 tech giants accounted for more than 16% of Fortune 500 earnings – even in a dwon year." *Fortune*. June 6, 2023.

_____. "Colgate Announces 4th Quarter 2019 Results." *Reuters*. January 31, 2020.

_____. "Should You Buy Colgate-Palmolive for It Incredibly Reliable Dividend?" *The Globe and Mail*. March 13, 2023.

Virtue, Graeme. "How we made Teenage Mutant Ninja Turtles." *The Guardian*. May 10, 2016.

Lammle, Rob. "The Complete History of Teenage Mutant Ninja Turtles." *Mental Floss*. June 27, 2015.

Li, Yun. "Investing legend Peter Lynch on the investments he regrets not making in recent years." *CNBC*. April 25, 2023.

_____. "Tom Monaghan: In 30 Minutes Or Less." *Entrepreneur*. October 10, 2008.

Trainer, David. "Domino's Pizza: Delivering A Superior Business Model." *Forbes*. March 28, 2022.

_____. "Domino's Pizza Announces Fourth Quarter And Fiscal 2022 Financial Results." *Domino's Pizza Website*. February 23, 2023.

Raye, Mike. "The Difference That Helps Domino's Deliver More Than Pizza." *The Motley Fool*. September 3, 2020.

Martin, Emmie. "Nicolas Cage once blew $150 million on a private island and a dinosaur skull – here's everything he bought." *CNBC*. January 20, 2018.

Yaged, Christine. "How Nicolas Cage Wildly Spent a $150 Million Fortune." *FinanceBuzz*. February 6, 2023.

Iyer, Radha. "Despite His $450 Million Net Worth, Arnold Schwarzenegger Doesn't Own Basic Necessity Due to His 'Big Thumbs.'" *EssentiallySports.com*. October 30, 2022.

Blackwell, Richard. "Remember when: What have we learned from the 1980s and that 21% interest rate?" *The Globe and Mail*. May 13, 2015.

Heaven, Pamela. "Posthaste: Why inflation-pinched Canadians aren't stuck in a return of 'That 70s show.'" *Financial Post.* May 24, 2022.

Taylor, Mac. "California's High Housing Costs: Causes and Consequences." *Legislative Analyst's Office.* March 17, 2015.

Jargon, Julie. "McDonald's Won't Spin Off Real Estate Holdings." *Wall Street Journal.* November 10, 2015.

Gravvat, Liam. "Number of McDonald's locations in the United States, North America and world in 2022." *USA Today.* July 30, 2022.

Egan, John. "McDonald's Long-Term Real Estate Structure Provides It with a Cushion Even in a Severe Downturn." *Wealth Management.com.* April 16, 2020.

Cutolo, Morgan. "Here's What Walmart Looked Like When It First Opened In 1962." *Readers Digest Magazine.* November 30, 2021.

Stevenson, Richard W. "Walton Heads List Of Richest in U.S." *The New York Times.* October 15, 1985.

Forbes Wealth Team. "Billion-Dollar Dynasties: These Are The Richest Families In America." *Forbes.* December 17, 2020.

Kohan, Shelley E. "Walmart Revenue Hits $559 Billion For Fiscal Year 2020." *Forbes.* February 18, 2021.

Cardenal, Andres. "Better Buy Now: Amazon.com or Wal-Mart Stores?" *The Motley Fool.* July 28, 2015.

McBride, Stephen. "Walmart Has Made A Genius Move To Beat Amazon." *Forbes.* January 8, 2020.

Niedt, Bob. "13 Reasons to Shop at Walmart (Even If You Hate Walmart)." *Kiplinger*. August 4, 2021.

Brock, Catherine. "Best REITS For Reliable Income For 2023." *Forbes*. June 27, 2023.

Frankel, Matthew. "The Vanguard REIT ETF: Growth and Income With Lower Risk Than Individual REITs." *The Motley Fool*. March 18, 2021.

_____. "Saudi Arabia's economy to exceed $1 trillion for first time in history: IMF estimate." *Al Arabiya News*. May 4, 2022.

_____. "Mar 3, 1938 CE: Oil Discovered in Saudi Arabia." *National Geographic Society*. August 9, 2022.

_____. "Saudi Aramco soars to $2 trillion on sky-high oil prices." *Al Jazeera*. October 6, 2021.

Olsen, Morten. "Vision 2030 Plan: Saudi Arabia post-oil?" *IESE Business School University of Navarra*. July 19, 2016.

_____. "Limits on OPEC Output Increase Global Oil Production Costs." *National Bureau of Economic Research*. January 2018.

_____. "Oil Sands Production versus Global Oil Prices." *C.D. Howe Institute*. January 19, 2023.

_____. "Despite Being World's 4th Largest Oil Producer, Majority of Crude Oil Demand in Canada is Met via the United States." *Business Wire*. August 11, 2021.

_____. "Canada's Suncor posts quarterly profit on improved crude prices." *Reuters*. July 28, 2021.

Handley, Lucy. "Puma has stuck with me through everything: Usain Bolt." *CNBC*. November 29, 2016.

Grant, Mitchell. "What Is Usain Bolt Worth?" *Investopedia*. May 5, 2019.

Tighe, D. "Gross profit margin percentage of Nike worldwide from 2014 to 2022." *Statista*. August 15, 2022.

_____. "Ford Motor Gross Margin 2010-2023." *MacroTrends*. March 31, 2023.

Badenhausen, Kurt. "How Michael Jordan Will Make $145 Million In 2019." *Forbes*. August 28, 2019.

_____. "Messi beats Ronaldo in 2019 Forbes rich list." *ESPN*. June 11, 2019.

Sturgeon, Jamie. "BCE, Rogers become Canada's newest odd couple." *Financial Post*. December 9, 2011.

_____. "BCE reports 2022 Q4 and full-year results, announces 2023 financial targets." *PR Newswire*. February 2, 2023.

_____. "BCE raises quarterly dividend as results nearly recover from COVID-19 pandemic." *City News*. February 3, 2022.

Smith, Nelson. "These 3 Dividend Kings Haven't Missed a Payout in 100 Years." *Yahoo! Finance*. December 15, 2019.

Cavendish, Richard. "George Stephenson's First Steam Locomotive." *History Today*. July 25, 2014.

Rothstein, Edward. "Looking at the Transcontinental Railroad as the Internet of 1869." *The New York Times*. December 11, 1999.

_____. "Cornelius Vanderbilt." *History*. April 16, 2010.

Ng, Kay. "Can CN Rail (TSX:CNR) Stock Double Your Money?" *The Motley Fool.* October 30, 2019.

Lowrie, Morgan. "Lac-Megantic marks 10th anniversary of train derailment that killed 47 people." *Global News.* July 6, 2023.

_____. "Warren Buffett's US$26.5-billion investment in this major railroad has turned into a cash machine." *Financial Post.* November 11, 2014.

_____. "We Go Beyond." *cnrail.com* July 20, 2023.

Gilchrist, Karen. "How Richard Branson started Virgin Atlantic with a blackboard selling $39 flights." *CNBC.* December 29, 2019.

Holmes, Frank. "What Headwinds? Airlines to Book Their 10th Straight Year of Profitability." *Forbes.* January 28, 2019.

Josephs, Leslie. "US airlines are losing money for the first time in years as coronavirus ends travel boom." *CNBC.* April 23, 2020.

Franck, Thomas. "Warren Buffett says Berkshire sold all its airline stocks because of the coronavirus." *CNBC.* May 2, 2020.

Fox, Matthew. "Hertz skyrockets 825% since filing for bankruptcy as Robinhood traders pile in." *Business Insider.* June 7, 2020.

Healy, Will. "Coca-Cola: Great Income Stock or Dividend Trap?" *Motley Fool.* Sept 3, 2023.

_____. "The Town of Coca-Cola Millionaires" *Ripley's Believe It or Not!.* Feb 8, 2023.

Printed in Canada